Doggin'
Northern Virginia

The 50 Best Places
To Hike With Your Dog
In NOVA

DOUG GELBERT

illustrations by

ANDREW CHESWORTH

Cruden Bay Books

There is always a new trail to look forward to...

DOGGIN' NORTHERN VIRGINIA: THE 50 BEST PLACES
TO HIKE WITH YOUR DOG IN NOVA

Copyright 2006 by Cruden Bay Books

Cruden Bay Books
PO Box 467
Montchanin, DE 19710
www.hikewithyourdog.com

International Standard Book Number 0978562240

"Dogs are our link to paradise...to sit with a dog on a hillside on a glorious afternoon is to be back in Eden, where doing nothing was not boring - it was peace."
- Milan Kundera

Ahead On The Trail

Introduction

Northern Virginia can be a great place to hike with your dog. Within an couple hours' drive from you can hike on sand trails, climb mountains that leave your dog panting, walk on some of the most historic grounds in America, explore the estates of America's wealthiest families or circle lakes for miles and never lose sight of the water.

I have selected what I consider to be the 50 best places to take your dog for an outing and ranked them according to subjective criteria including the variety of hikes available, opportunities for canine swimming and pleasure of the walks. The rankings include a mix of parks that feature long walks and parks that contain short walks. Did I miss your favorite? Let us know at *www.hikewithyourdog.com.*

For dog owners it is important to realize that not all parks are open to our best trail companions (see page 14 for a list of parks that do not allow dogs). It is sometimes hard to believe but not everyone loves dogs. We are, in fact, in the minority when compared with our non-dog owning neighbors.

So when visiting a park always keep your dog under control and clean up any messes and we can all expect our great parks to remain open to our dogs. And maybe some others will see the light as well. *Remember, every time you go out with your dog you are an ambassador for all dog owners.*

Grab that leash and hit the trail!
DBG

Hiking With Your Dog

So you want to start hiking with your dog. Hiking with your dog can be a fascinating way to explore Northern Virginia from a canine perspective. Some things to consider:

❀ Dog's Health

Hiking can be a wonderful preventative for any number of physical and behavioral disorders. One in every three dogs is overweight and running up trails and leaping through streams is great exercise to help keep pounds off. Hiking can also relieve boredom in a dog's routine and calm dogs prone to destructive habits. And hiking with your dog strengthens the overall owner/dog bond.

❀ Breed of Dog

All dogs enjoy the new scents and sights of a trail. But some dogs are better suited to hiking than others. If you don't as yet have a hiking companion, select a breed that matches your interests. Do you look forward to an entire afternoon's hiking? You'll need a dog bred to keep up with such a pace, such as a retriever or a spaniel. Is a half-hour enough walking for you? It may not be for an energetic dog like a border collie. If you already have a hiking friend, tailor your plans to his abilities.

❀ Conditioning

Just like humans, dogs need to be acclimated to the task at hand. An inactive dog cannot be expected to bounce from the easy chair in the den to complete a 3-hour hike. You must also be physically able to restrain your dog if confronted with distractions on the trail (like a scampering squirrel or a pack of joggers). Have your dog checked by a veterinarian before significantly increasing his activity level.

❀ Weather

Hot humid summers do not do dogs any favors. With no sweat glands and only panting available to disperse body heat, dogs are much more susceptible to heat stroke than we are. Unusually rapid panting and/or a bright red tongue are signs of heat exhaustion in your pet.

Always carry enough water for your hike. Even days that don't seem too warm can cause discomfort in dark-coated dogs if the sun is shining brightly. In cold weather, short-coated breeds may require additional attention.

❖ Trail Hazards

Dogs won't get poison ivy but they can transfer it to you. Stinging nettle is a nuisance plant that lurks on the side of many trails and the slightest brush will deliver troublesome needles into a dog's coat. Some trails are littered with small pieces of broken glass that can slice a dog's paws. Nasty thorns can also blanket trails that we in shoes may never notice.

❖ Ticks

You won't be able to spend much time in Virginia parks without encountering ticks. All are nasty but the deer tick - no bigger than a pin head - carries with it the spectre of Lyme disease. Lyme disease attacks a dog's joints and makes walking painful. The tick needs to be embedded in the skin to transmit Lyme disease. It takes 4-6 hours for a tick to become embedded and another 24-48 hours to transmit Lyme disease bacteria.

When hiking, walk in the middle of trails away from tall grass and bushes. And when the summer sun fades away don't stop thinking about ticks - they remain active any time the temperature is above 30 degrees. By checking your dog - and yourself - thoroughly after each walk you can help avoid Lyme disease. Ticks tend to congregate on your dog's ears, between the toes and around the neck and head.

❖ Water

Surface water, including fast-flowing streams, is likely to be infested with a microscopic protozoa called *Giardia*, waiting to wreak havoc on a dog's intestinal system. The most common symptom is crippling diarrhea. Algae, pollutants and contaminants can all be in streams, ponds and puddles. If possible, carry fresh water for your dog on the trail - your dog can even learn to drink happily from a squirt bottle.

Rattlesnakes and Copperheads

Rattlesnakes and their close cousins, copperheads, are not particularly aggressive animals but you should treat any venomous snake with respect and keep your distance. A rattler's colors may vary but they are recognized by the namesake rattle on the tail and a diamond-shaped head. Unless cornered or teased by humans or dogs, a rattlesnake will crawl away and avoid striking. Avoid placing your hand in unexamined rocky areas and crevasses and try and keep your dog from doing so as well. If you hear a nearby rattle, stop immediately and hold your dog back. Identify where the snake is and slowly back away.

If you or your dog is bitten, do not panic but get to a hospital or veterinarian with as little physical movement as possible. Wrap between the bite and the heart. Rattlesnakes might give "dry bites" where no poison is injected, but you should always check with a doctor after a bite even if you feel fine.

Black Bears

Are you likely to see a bear while out hiking with your dog? No, it's not likely. It is, however, quite a thrill if you are fortunate enough to spot a black bear on the trail - from a distance.

Black bear attacks are incredibly rare. In the year 2000 a hiker was killed by a black bear in Great Smoky National Park and it was the first deadly bear attack in the 66-year history of America's most popular national park. It was the first EVER in the southeastern United States. In all of North America only 43 black bear mauling deaths have ever been recorded (through 1999).

Most problems with black bears occur near a campground (like the above incident) where bears have learned to forage for unprotected food. On the trail bears will typically see you and leave the area. What should you do if you encounter a black bear? Experts agree on three important things:

1) Never run. A bear will outrun you, outclimb you, outswim you. Don't look like prey.
2) Never get between a female bear and a cub who may be nearby feeding.
3) Leave a bear an escape route.

If the bear is at least 15 feet away and notices you make sure you keep your dog close and calm. If a bear stands on its hind legs or comes closer it may just be trying to get a better view or smell to evaluate the situation. Wave your arms and make noise to scare the bear away. Most bears will quickly leave the area.

If you encounter a black bear at close range, stand upright and make yourself appear as large a foe as possible. Avoid direct eye contact and speak in a calm, assertive and assuring voice as you back up slowly and out of danger.

Porcupines

Porcupines are easy for a curious dog to catch and that makes them among the most dangerous animals you may meet because an embedded quill is not only painful but can cause infection if not properly removed.

Outfitting Your Dog For A Hike

These are the basics for taking your dog on a hike:

▸ **Collar.**
It should not be so loose as to come off but you should be able to slide your flat hand under the collar.

▸ **Identification Tags.**
Get one with your veterinarian's phone number as well.

▸ **Bandanna.**
Can help distinguish him from game in hunting season.

▸ **Leash.**
Leather lasts forever but if there's water in your dog"s future, consider quick-drying nylon.

▸ **Water.**
Carry 8 ounces for every hour of hiking.

🐾 *I want my dog to help carry water, snacks and other supplies on the trail. Where do I start?*
To select an appropriate dog pack measure your dog's girth around the rib cage. A dog pack should fit securely without hindering the dog's ability to walk normally.

🐾 *Will my dog wear a pack?*
Wearing a dog pack is no more obtrusive than wearing a collar, although some dogs will take to a pack easier than others. Introduce the pack by draping a towel over your dog's back in the house and then having your dog wear an empty pack on short walks. Progressively add some crumpled newspaper and then bits of clothing. Fill the pack with treats and reward your dog from the stash. Soon your dog will associate the dog pack with an outdoor adventure and will eagerly look forward to wearing it.

🐾 *How much weight can I put into a dog pack?*

Many dog packs are sold by weight recommendations. A healthy, well-conditioned dog can comfortably carry 25% to 33% of its body weight. Breeds prone to back problems or hip dysplasia should not wear dog packs. Consult your veterinarian before stuffing the pouches with gear.

🐾 *How does a dog wear a pack?*

The pack, typically with cargo pouches on either side, should ride as close to the shoulders as possible without limiting movement. The straps that hold the dog pack in place should be situated where they will not cause chafing.

🐾 *What are good things to put in a dog pack?*

Low density items such as food and poop bags are good choices. Ice cold bottles of water can cool your dog down on hot days. Don't put anything in a dog pack that can break. Dogs will bang the pack on rocks and trees as they wiggle through tight spots in the trail. Dogs also like to lie down in creeks and other wet spots so seal items in plastic bags. A good use for dog packs when on day hikes around Northern Virginia is trail maintenance - your dog can pack out trash left by inconsiderate visitors before you.

❖ *Are dog booties a good idea?*

Dog booties can be an asset, especially for the occasional canine hiker whose paw pads have not become toughened. Some trails around Norhern Virginia involve rocky terrain. In some places, there may be broken glass. Hiking boots for dogs are designed to prevent pads from cracking while trotting across rough surfaces. Used in winter, dog booties provide warmth and keep ice balls from forming between toe pads when hiking through snow.

❖ *What should a doggie first aid kit include?*

Even when taking short hikes it is a good idea to have some basics available for emergencies:

▸ 4" square gauze pads
▸ cling type bandaging tapes
▸ topical wound disinfectant cream
▸ tweezers
▸ insect repellent - no reason to leave your dog unprotected against mosquitoes and blackflies
▸ veterinarian's phone number

"I can't think of anything that brings me closer to tears than when my old dog - completely exhausted afters a hard day in the field - limps away from her nice spot in front of the fire and comes over to where I'm sitting and puts her head in my lap, a paw over my knee, and closes her eyes, and goes back to sleep. I don't know what I've done to deserve that kind of friend."
-Gene Hill

Low Impact Hiking With Your Dog

Every time you hike with your dog on the trail you are an ambassador for all dog owners. Some people you meet won't believe in your right to take a dog on the trail. Be friendly to all and make the best impression you can by practicing low impact hiking with your dog:

- Pack out everything you pack in.

- Do not leave dog scat on the trail; if you haven't brought plastic bags for poop removal bury it away from the trail and topical water sources.

- Hike only where dogs are allowed.

- Stay on the trail.

- Do not allow your dog to chase wildlife.

- Step off the trail and wait with your dog while horses and other hikers pass.

- Do not allow your dog to bark - people are enjoying the trail for serenity.

- *Have as much fun on your hike as your dog does.*

The Other End Of The Leash

Leash laws are like speed limits - everyone seems to have a private interpretation of their validity. Some dog owners never go outside with an unleashed dog; others treat the laws as suggestions or disregard them completely. It is not the purpose of this book to tell dog owners where to go to evade the leash laws or reveal the parks where rangers will look the other way at an unleashed dog. Nor is it the business of this book to preach vigilant adherence to the leash laws. Nothing written in a book is going to change people's behavior with regard to leash laws. So this will be the last time leash laws are mentioned, save occasionally when we point out the parks where dogs are welcomed off leash.

How To Pet A Dog
Tickling tummies slowly and gently works wonders.
Never use a rubbing motion; this makes dogs bad-tempered.
A gentle tickle with the tips of the fingers is all that is necessary
to induce calm in a dog. I hate strangers who go up to dogs with their
hands held to the dog's nose, usually palm towards themselves.
How does the dog know that the hand doesn't hold something horrid?
The palm should always be shown to the dog and go straight
down to between the dog's front legs and tickle gently with
a soothing voice to accompany the action.
Very often the dog raises its back leg in a scratching movement,
it gets so much pleasure from this.
-Barbara Woodhouse

No Dogs

Before we get started on the best places to take your dog, let's get out of the way some of the trails that do not allow dogs:

Fairfax County
Fraser Preserve
Winkler Botanical Preserve

Fauquier County
Wildcat Mountain Natural Area
Sandy Point State Park

Prince William County
Bull Run Mountain State Natural Area
Occoquan Bay National Wildlife Refuge

O.K. that wasn't too bad. Let's forget about these and move on to some of the great places where we CAN take our dogs across Northern Virginia...

10 Cool Things To See On Northern Virginia Trails With Your Dog

"If your dog is fat," the old saying goes, "you aren't getting enough exercise." But walking the dog need not be just about a little exercise. Here are 10 cool things you can see in Northern Virginia while out walking the dog.

🐾 HISTORIC GRAVEYARDS

In **Fountainhead Regional Park** the Davis family cemetery, anchored by a majestic white oak, pops up in the woods just a few steps into the canine hike on both the white and blue trails. The graveyard was established in the 1860s. At **Leesylvania State Park** is the original hilltop resting place of prominent Lee family members and at **Ball's Bluff Regional Park** is one of the smallest national cemeteries in America with only the remains of 54 Union soldiers from the Civil War.

🐾 HIGH WATER MARKS

In **Great Falls Park** is a High Water Mark Pole that records the depths to which the Potomac far below can flood. The most recent marking is from January 21, 1996 when the river rose 85 feet in 48 hours. That mark is about eye-high to a beagle - it was only the fifth largest flood of the past 100 years. For the highest mark you'll have to look overhead to see where the waters ot the Great Potomac Flood of 1936 reached.

🐾 OUR NATIONAL BIRD

Mason Neck has been named one of the Top Ten sites in America for viewing bald eagles. The eagles arrive in October and spend the next two months courting and breeding where they are visible feeding in the marsh. By February they have re-built their nests and are ready to lay eggs. The eaglets hatch in April and spend the next several months gaining strength before the cycle begins anew. Eagles can be viewed on trails in **Mason Neck State Park** and **Mason Neck National Wildlife Refuge**.

EARLY INDUSTRIAL SOUVENIRS

In the center of the **Occoquan Regional Park** is the last of nine bee-hive brick kilns that were used by prisoners to churn out many of the red bricks used in Northern Virginia buildings. Along the **Potomac Heritage Trail** are the rusty hulks of 19th-century boilers used to quarry Potomac bluestone. This 500-million year old schist was a popular building stone for many buildings around Northwest Washington, including the Old Stone House in Georgetown, built in 1765. Several of the animal houses in the National Zoo use Potomac bluestone, the Panda House and the Elephant House are just two.

INSPIRATIONAL MONUMENTS

Nestled in the center of **Theodore Roosevelt Island** is a 17-foot bronze statue by Paul Manship. The memorial overlooks a diorama of fountains and four 21-foot granite tablets, inscribed with the tenets of the 26th President's thoughts on Nature, Youth, Manhood and the State.

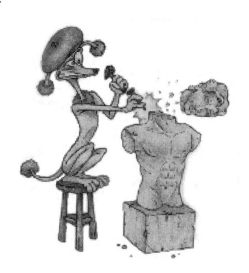

A CARPET OF BLUE

The *Bluebell Walk* begins on the Nature Trail near the Visitor Center of **Bull Run Regional Park** and makes its way to the confluence of Cub Run and Bull Run. This is a meandering 1.5-mile canine hike through the largest stand of bluebells on the East Coast. In springtime the display on the forest floor is unforgettable.

BIG WILDFLOWERS

The *Trillium rhomboideum* variety *grandiflorum* was given its name by french botanist Andre Michaux in 1803. The specific name, very appropriately means "large-flowered." Sometimes called Snow Trillium because it is the first trillium to bloom and therefore would be caught in a late snowfall, the white-flowered plants (the petals turn pink with age) prefer to inhabit slopes 1,000-3,500 feet in elevation. Of the 10 or so species of trillium in the Blue Ridge, *grandiflorum* may be the most abundant. The largest colony in the country can be found in the G. Richard Thompson Wildlife Management Area, where an estimated 18 million plants thrive.

ANCIENT FOOTPATHS

The last known undeveloped section of the historic Vestal's Gap Road runs across Claude Moore Park. This trail, first used by American Indians, was used as early as 1692 by the Rangers of the Potomac under David Strahan. It became the major route for travel between Alexandria and Winchester. George Washington used the road frequently in his travels between Mount Vernon and the western frontier. Major General Edward Braddock's troops, including Daniel Boone, traveled Vestal's Gap Road during the French and Indian War and today your dog can hike a short ways on the ancient thoroughfare.

WELL-BUILT BRIDGES

The bridge across the Accotink Creek linking the trail system in Accotink Bay Wildlife Refuge was built by D Company of the 11th Engineer Battalion. The unit was activated during World War I to maintain railroads in northern France and in August 1917 was the first American unit to enter the European theater. Until World War II the regiment conducted numerous missions over the rugged terrain and dense jungles of the Panama Canal Zone and adopted the nickname "Jungle Cats." This bridge is a suspension bridge in the manner of the famous Brooklyn Bridge.

🐾 OLD MINES

In Prince William Forest Park, if you head off on the *North Valley Trail* and continue about one mile down the *Pyrite Mine Trail* along the North Branch of the Quantico Creek you will reach the remains of the Cabin Branch Pyrite Mine. The mine opened in 1889, pulling nugget-like rocks known as "fool's gold" for their appearance to the precious metal. In fact pyrite is loaded with sulfur (needed to make gunpowder) that kept the operation profitable into the 1920s, including an important stretch during World War I when as many as 300 men worked the mine. Many acres of historic underground workings, pilings and foundations have been reclaimed by the Park Service and are remembered today.

The 50 Best Places To Hike With Your Dog In Northern Virginia...

1

Sky Meadows State Park

The Park

It was 1731 when James Ball picked up 7.883 acres on the eastern slopes of the Blue Ridge Mountain from Lord Fairfax. Over the years through inheritance the land was divided and divided and divided. In 1966 a housing development was planned that called for further division into 50-acre lots.

At this Point Paul Mellon stepped in and eventually donated 1,132 acres that became Sky Meadows State Park in 1983. Mellon was happy enough with the results to donate an additional 462 acres across Route 17 that had originally been purchased by George Washington from Lord Fairfax.

Fauquier

Phone Number
- (540) 592-3556

Website
- www.dcr.state.va.us/parks/skymeado.htm

Admission Fee
- Yes, single day pass required

Park Hours
- 8 a.m. to dusk

Directions
- The park is south of Paris. From Route 50 turn left on Route 17 South to park entrance on right. From I-66, take Exit 23 on Route 17 North seven miles to the park entrance on left.

The Walks

When you place your park on the Blue Ridge mountain slopes far removed from eight-lane roads clogged with traffic you have to work hard not to be the best place to hike with your dog in Northern Virginia and Sky Meadows does not disappoint. The real star here are the meadows - there simply aren't many open-air hikes available across Northern Virginia. Be advised, however, that if you've never gone much beyond your neighborhood walk with your dog, this isn't the place for your first big adventure. Except for the *Snowden Trail* nature loop you will be hiking up a mountain at Sky Meadows.

The trail system offers about ten miles of marked paths that can be molded into canine hiking loops, the most popular being the North Ridge-South Ridge circuit. The *South Ridge Trail* utilizes an old farm road while the *North Ridge Trail* picks its way up the mountain like a traditional hiking trail. You are

probably best served by going up the South Ridge since it is not as steep and are longer coming down the North side.

For those looking for a full day of hiking with your dog the *Appalachian Trail* is 1.7 miles away and there are loop options up there as well. If you just want to enjoy the meadows you can confine your explorations to the *Piedmont Overlook Trail* on the North Ridge. It is also possible to enjoy the park without hard climbing on the Snowden Trail interpretive nature walk and the *Shearman's Mill Trail*.

Trail Sense: There is a trail map, the paths are blazed and there are directional signs with distances at trail junctions.

Dog Friendliness
Dogs are not permitted on the bridle trails but can stay in the campground for an additional $3.00.

Traffic
The hiking trails are for pedestrian use only.

Canine Swimming
There are seasonal streams on the mountain and a reedy three-acre pond off Route 17 to refresh your dog after a hearty hike.

Trail Time
Several hours to a full day.

2
Mason Neck
State Park

The Park

In the 1960s, after it was determined that the widespread use of the pesticide DDT was decimating bald eagle populations by weakening their eggshells, a nesting pair was spotted on Mason Neck. The Mason Neck Conservation Committee was formed to protect the area. A plan for a state park was hatched and the Commonwealth began purchasing land on the peninsula in 1967.

The group's mettle was tested immediately as they helped rebuff a steady parade of proposed development projects: a beltway, an airport, pipelines, a landfill. The long-dreamed-of state park finally opened for public use in 1985.

The Walks

There are a half-dozen canine hiking options in Mason Neck State Park,

Fairfax

Phone Number
- (703) 339-2380

Website
- www.dcr.state.va.us/parks/ma-sonnec.htm

Admission Fee
- Yes, vehicle entrance fee

Hours
- 8:00 a.m. to sunset

Directions
- From I-95 exit into Lorton on Route 642 East. Turn right on Route 1 (Richmond Highway) and left on Route 242 (Gunston Road). Continue on Route 600 past Gunston Plantation, making a right onto High Point Road at the sign for Mason Neck State Park/National Refuge and follow to park.

the stars being three loop trails of about one mile in length. All run easily through an attractive oak/holly forest on paw-friendly soft dirt and are pretty enough you will want to complete them all. You can actually use the *Wilson Spring Trail*, marked in yellow, to access them all with a bit of backtracking.

The red-blazed *Bay View Trail* skips across two inlets from Belmont Bay and offers splendid open-water vistas and close-up looks at the marsh with its turtles and frogs. Mason Neck is a delight for your dog in any season but you may want to remember the wintertime for yourself when the leaves drop from the trees to allow easier sights of eagles diving for fish in the bay.

Trail Sense: A trail map is available and the paths are marked with signs and energetically blazed with metal markers.

Pollution in the Potomac River killed most of the plants in the Belmont Bay that has led to the erosion of the shoreline in Mason Neck State Park.

Dog Friendliness
Dogs are welcome throughout the park.

Traffic
This is a lightly visited place. The trails are for foot traffic only; bikes are allowed only on the paved *High Point Multi-Use Trail* that runs the length of the peninsula.

Canine Swimming
It doesn't get any better for dogs than on the beach at the Belmont Bay off the Bay View Trail.

Trail Time
More than an hour.

3
Prince William Forest Park

The Park

This was some of the earliest European-settled land in the country. Early tobacco farming in the area drained the land of much of its nutrients and for centuries only a few farms survived around the creeks flowing into the Potomac River. During the Depression of the 1930s this was one of 46 locations of marginal farm land selected to be developed for recreation. Prince William Forest became a part of the National Park System in 1940 and work camps from the Civilian Conservation Corps were established to build roads and trails and bridges. Five rustic cabin camps built at this time are listed on the National Register of Historic Places.

Prince William

Phone Number
- (703) 221-7181

Website
- www.nps.gov/prwi/

Admission Fee
- None

Park Hours
- 9:00 a.m. - 5:00 p.m.

Directions
- Located 35 miles south of Washington, DC. Take I-95 to exit 150 (Joplin Road/VA Route 619). Take Route 619 West to the park entrance road (approximately 1/4 mile).

The Walks

At over 15,000 acres, Prince William Forest Park is the largest protected swath of land in the Washington DC metropolitan area. Although just south of the nation's capital in this densely populated area, the trails in the forest are refreshingly uncrowded - always an attraction for canine hikers.

The canine hiking here is through the only preserved Eastern Piedmont forest in the National Park Service. You will be working up and down and around the many slopes in the Quantico Creek watershed - often with long views through the forest that features little understory in many areas. Many of the trails lead away from Scenic Drive to the South Branch and the North Branch of Quantico Creek.

In addition to the wide, well-marked hiking trails you can take off on several old access roads that deliver a country-lane feel to the hiking. You can also use the paved - but walkable - Scenic Drive to close some of your customized loops.

Trail Sense: Directions and distances on posts at the many trail junctions make it easy to carve any hiking outing with your dog here.

Dog Friendliness

Turkey Run Ridge Group Campground and the Chopawamsic Backcountry Area.

Traffic

As you motor around the Scenic Drive loop the dozen or so parking lots at trailheads scarcely have space for ten vehicles each. That makes these 37 miles of trails a prime destination for a lively dog.

Canine Swimming

These gurgling brooks have been colonized by beavers, once decimated in the area but recovering from a single pair introduced some years ago, whose dams have created small pools just deep enough for a good canine swim.

Trail Time

A visit to Prince William Forest can easily consume a full day.

4
Great Falls Park

The Park

To George Washington the Great Falls of the Potomac were an obstacle that needed to be overcome to open the Ohio Valley to lucrative trade. The Patowmack Company was chartered in 1784 to construct a laborious series of five canals that were completed in 1802. It was considered the greatest engineering feat in early America.

The canal prospered for only a quarter-century. In the early 1900s John McLean and Steven Elkins acquired the lands surrounding Great Falls and built an amusement park. Tourists traveled along a trolley from Georgetown to the park to see the hydrospectacular in the rocky river. The venture was an immediate success but eventually fell victim to the intermittent flooding of the Potomac.

Potomac Edison Power Company came along with plans to construct a hydroelectric dam here but the area geology could not be tamed to complete the project. Finally in 1966, through an agreement with Fairfax County, the National Park Service acquired 800 acres of land to create Great Falls Park.

Fairfax

Phone Number
- (703) 285-2965

Website
- www.nps.gov/grfa/index.htm

Admission Fee
- Yes, a 3-day pass whether on foot or in a vehicle; annual pass available

Park Hours
- 7:00 a.m. to dark

Directions
- Take Beltway Exit 44 for Route 193, Georgetown Pike, and head west. About three miles down the road, you will come to a traffic light at Old Dominion Drive where you will see a sign for the park. Make a right at the light. Old Dominion Drive will deadend at the entrance station, about one mile down the road.

The Walks

The star canine hike at Great Falls is the *River Trail* that will take your dog to the edge of the 79-foot falls and the steep-walled Mather Gorge. The path travels through the remains of Matildaville, a thriving town from the long-ago canal age, as well as remnants of the Patowmack Canal. The blue-blazed trail twists through a rocky alpine-like environment not often seen in Northern Virginia.

Another unique habitat in the park - also hiker-only - is the *Swamp Trail* that explores an ancient terrace of the Potomac River for about one mile. Your dog will enjoy the level terrain and multiple stream crossings on this ramble.

The bulk of the park's 15 miles of trails are on old carriage roads and roadbeds that also allow horses and sometimes bikes. But these routes are wide and well-graded that make for an excellent canine hike. The trails slip under quiet treetops and historic structures.

Trail Sense: There are excellent trail maps and plenty of signage out on the trails.

Dog Friendliness

Dogs are allowed throughout the park.

Traffic

There are trails for foot traffic only; trails for horses, dogs and people, and trails for hikers/bikers/horses.

Canine Swimming

Don't let your dog try it.

Trail Time

Up to a half-day and more is possible.

5
The Battlefields
of Manassas

The Park

The Manassas Gap and the Orange and Alexandria railroads crossed in Manassas, a surveyor's decision in the 1850s that would transform this small farming community into one of America's best-known towns. Twice in the first two years of the Civil War the Northern and Southern armies clashed five miles north of town near a creek called Bull Run, resulting in 30,000 casualties in an attempt to control that railroad junction.

On July 21, 1861 the Civil War was expected to end. The fully-equipped Union Army under General Irvin McDowell was prepared to take the field for the first time at Bull Run. The complete submission of the rebels was such a certainty the Federal troops were accompanied by picnickers and sightseers. After ten hours of bloody fighting the Union Army was in retreat towards Washington and it was apparent this was not going to be a one-battle war.

The armies returned to Bull Run a year later, seasoned and spirited. Robert E. Lee's Army of Northern Virginia was at the peak of its power and he outmaneuvered General John Pope's Union

Prince William

Phone Number
- (703) 361-1339

Website
- www.nps.gov/mana/

Admission Fee
- Daily and season passes available

Park Hours
- Dawn to dusk

Directions
- Travel west on I-66 to Exit 47B, Route 234 North (Sudley Road). Proceed through the first traffic light. The entrance to the Henry Hill Visitors Center is on the right, just past the Northern Virginia Community College.

army in three days of struggle beginning August 28. With his masterful victory here Lee was able to carry the war to the North for the first time.

The Walks

The main canine hiking here is on two trails that interpret the two critical Civil War clashes over this ground. Each route covers more than five miles and offers a pleasing mix of open-field and woods hiking. Expect the fields - that retain much of its wartime character - to be muddy in times of wet weather. The moderate terrain and abundance of interpretive markers makes the lengthy hikes go by easier.

The *First Manassas Trail* takes in Bull Run and the Stone Bridge where the first shots were fired. It also features more open fields. The *Second Manassas Trail* across the western section of the park is the preferred route to take your dog on a busy day. If time is limited take the one-mile *Henry Hill Loop Trail* around the Visitor Center where the critical fighting in the first battle of the Civil War took place. The trail follows part of the Southern Line where General Thomas J. Jackson received his immortal nickname "Stonewall."

Trail Sense: The National Park map gets you pointed in the right direction and the trail junctions are well-marked. There are also plenty of unmarked hiking trails across the battlefields to explore.

Dog Friendliness

Dogs are allowed throughout the park.

Traffic

Bicycles are banned from the trails; some of the trails support horse travel. Most visitors opt for the auto tour so there is seldom much competition for the walking paths. Your main concern will be shepherding your dog across the busy roadways on the bigger hikes.

Canine Swimming

There are a few streams and Bull Run can pool deep enough for a little swim.

Trail Time

You could spend a full day traipsing across the battlefield.

6
Claude Moore Park

The Park

The park in eastern Loudoun County includes parts of two land grants made by Lord Fairfax in 1729. The Lanesville House, built in the late 1700s, was used by travelers and as a post office.

In 1941 Dr. Claude Moore purchased the property at auction from the family who had lived here for 170 years. In 1975 he donated the property to the National Wildlife Federation.

In 1986 the NWF sold the property to developers and Moore, then in his 90s, was forced to initiate lawsuits to save the land that went all the way to the Virginia Supreme Court.

He lost all his appeals but county residents passed a bond referendum to purchase the site and preserve one of the last remaining greenspaces in a vast area of houses and box stores. A year after the park opened in 1990, Moore, still living on the property, passed away at the age of 98.

Loudoun

Phone Number
- (703) 444-1275

Website
- www.co.loudoun.va.us/prcs/
parks/claude.htm

Admission Fee
- None

Park Hours
- Dawn to dusk

Directions
- From the Beltway (I-495), take Route 7 West and exit at Cascades Parkway South. Immediately get into left lane and stay on Cascades Parkway South for approximately ½ mile. You will go through two lights. After the second light, the first entrance to the park is on your left. Enter here for the nature area. If comng from the south the nature area is the second entrance on the right.

The Walks

Claude Moore Park serves up a pastiche of a dozen short trails that add up to more than ten miles of canine hiking. Two trails - the white-blazed *Little Stoney Mountain Trail* and the blue-blazed *Scout Trail* - both follow essentially the same route to explore the entire park so you only have to choose one.

A popular destination for first-time visitors is the scenic overlook at the north end of the park on Little Stoney Mountain (at 442 feet, the hill's name

30

dates to a 1779 survey map). The cobblestones your dog has to negotiate on this stretch of trail are pre-historic souvenirs from wave action ten thousand years ago, when the Potomac River washed against this hill. The scenic view is of the monolithic Sugarloaf Mountain in Maryland (another great place to take your dog hiking).

Among the short trails around the Visitor's Center, the purple-blazed *Cedar Grove Trail* is a standout. For open-air hiking in the sunshine explore the trails around the ponds at the center of the park but don't let your dog into the water.

Trail Sense: A trail map is available and the paths are marked with signs and energetically blazed with metal markers.

Dog Friendliness
Dogs are welcome in the park but not on guided pro-grams such as the moonlight walks.

Traffic
Bikes are permitted only on paved and gravel roads and not on the hiking trails. No horses use the park.

Canine Swimming
Dogs are not permitted in the ponds and there are no streams to play in.

Trail Time
More than an hour.

7
Fountainhead Regional Park

The Park

As far back as the 1950s, visionaries in Fairfax County began preserving watershed land along the northern banks of the Occoquan River. Eventually they acquired more than 5,000 acres, creating a green necklace of regional parks. Fountainhead, at the confluence of Bull Run and the Occoquan is the keystone of those efforts.

With the population of the Occoquan watershed inching towards a half-million people dependent on the fresh water from the river, Fairfax County's actions seem downright prescient. Conversely, across the river the land was developed in Prince William County that now puts pressure on the region's drinking water supply.

Fairfax

Phone Number
- (703) 250-9124

Website
- www.nvrpa.org/fountainhead.html

Admission Fee
- None

Park Hours
- Dawn to dusk; closes after Thanksgiving for the winter

Directions
- Take I-95 south of the Beltway, exit at Occoquan and travel north on Route 123 approximately 5 miles. Turn left onto Hampton Road and drive 3 miles to the entrance on the left.

The Walks

Fountainhead is a trail user's park. Equestrian trails cover the eastern section down to the reservoir, mountain bikers have their own eight miles of wooded paradise and those traveling under their own power have plenty to smile about as well. The white-blazed pedestrian trail is a snaking, two-mile excursion around wide ravines and through airy woods. The hard-packed dirt path can be rooty in places so keep your dog high-stepping.

For real canine adventures you can set out on the 18-mile *Bull Run-Occoquan Trail*. Fountainhead is the southern terminus for the scenic, long-distance hike. If you just intend to sample the trail you'll find the Fountainhead leg to be a hilly exploration (sporty enough to require a switchback and wooden steps) of a finger of the Occoquan Reservoir. The trail, wide enough for a pack of dogs

in most places, is beautifully maintained by the Potomac Appalachian trail Club.

Trail Sense: There is a mapboard at the parking lot to get you oriented and the trails are well-blazed. Signs identify the differnet trailheads entering the woods from the parking lot.

Dog Friendliness

Dogs are allowed on all Fountainhead trails save for the mountain bike trail where no foot traffic is permitted.

Traffic

Surprisingly light given the quality of these trails; horses are allowed on the Bull Run-Occoquan Trail but no bikes.

Canine Swimming

No swimming in the Occoquan Reservoir.

Trail Time

Anywhere from an hour to a full day if you set out up the Bull Run-Occoquan Trail.

8
Leesylvania
State Park

The Park

Henry Lee II, great-grandfather of Robert E. Lee, named this property Leesylvania, or "Lee's Woods." These bluffs above the Potomac River had been in the Lee family for four generations but no one had thought to live here until Henry Lee moved to the site with his bride Lucy Grimes (who had spurned a young George Washington's romantic advances) in 1753.

In 1825 Leesylvania was sold out of the Lee family but Robert E. Lee would direct the building of a Confederate battery at his ancestral home during the Civil War. When the war ended the property fell into decline. A railroad line from Washington to Richmond was built past the old fort that eventually lured wealthy sportsmen who developed a hunting camp here.

In the 1950s entrepreneur Carl Hill ingeniously took advantage of an ancient grant to Lord Baltimore in 1632 that gave rights to the Potomac River to Maryland. He built a pier out into the river and anchored a 200-foot cruise ship at its end for use as a floating nightclub and gambling spot - liquor and gambling both being illegal in Virginia at the time. Freestone Point opened as the "Pleasureland of the East" in 1957. But a gambling emporium in the shadow of Washington, DC was not going to rake in money unnoticed. Legislation was passed to doom Hill's slot parlor and he sold the land to the American-Hawaiian Steamship Company, owned by Daniel K. Ludwig.

The reclusive Ludwig, tagged in his biography as the "Invisible Billionaire," was an admirer of the Lee legacy and donated the land to the Commonwealth for a state park. Leesylvania opened in 1992.

Prince William

Phone Number
- (703) 730-8205

Website
- www.state.va.us/dcr/parks/leesylva.htm

Admission Fee
- Yes, vehicle entrance fee

Directions
- From I-95, take Rippon Landing Exit 156; then go east on Route 784 to US 1. From US 1, follow Route 610 (Neabsco Road) east two miles.

The Walks

There are three loops to enjoy with your dog in Leesylvania - the star being the *Lee's Woods Trail*. This canine hike packs history aplenty into its two sporty miles atop the bluffs overlooking the Potomac River. Look for the brick fireplace that is the only reminder of the hunting lodge, earthwork gun placements from the Civil War battery, foundations from the plantation home and a family cemetery all located along the old stony dirt roads used for this trail.

Powells Creek Trail leads to long views across the water through woodlands away from the recreation areas of the park. For easy hiking with your dog take the *Potomac Trail* as it weaves through the former waterside amusement park that was part of the gambling gambit.

Trail Sense: A trail map is available and the trails are well-marked - but stay alert as the interpretive Lee's Woods Trail doubles back on itself in places.

Dog Friendliness

Dogs are allowed on the trails but not on the fishing pier.

Traffic

While the park can get busy, the trails seldom do. Hiking trails are for pedestrians only.

Canine Swimming

The beach around Free Stone Point is an ideal spot for a dog swim.

Trail Time

Up to a half-day to cover the trails and absorb the history of Leesylvania.

9
Harpers Ferry
National Historic Park

The Park

Few places in America pack as much scenic wonder and historical importance into such a small area as Harpers Ferry National Historic Park where the Shenandoah and Potomac rivers join forces. George Washington surveyed here as a young man. Thomas Jefferson hailed the confluence as "one of the most stupendous scenes in Nature" and declared it worth a trip across the Atlantic Ocean just to see. Meriwether Lewis prepared for the Corps of Discovery in 1804 by gathering supplies of arms and military stores at Harpers Ferry. A United States Marine Colonel named Robert E. Lee captured abolitionist John Brown at Harpers Ferry when he attempted to raid the United States Arsenal and arm a slave insurrection. General Thomas "Stonewall" Jackson scored one of his greatest military victories here during the Civil War.

Congress appropriated funds for a national monument in Harpers Ferry in 1944 and 2,300 acres of Maryland, Virginia and West Virginia were interwoven into the National Historic Park in 1963.

Loudoun

Phone Number
- (304) 535-6029

Website
- www.nps.gov/hafe/

Admission Fee
- None on the Maryland side

Directions
- To reach Maryland Heights, take the last left off of Route 340 before crossing the Potomac River. Turn right on Sandy Hook Road and continue to the parking area across from Harpers Ferry along the C & O Canal.

The Walks

Dogs are welcome in Harpers Ferry National Historic Park and hikes are available for every taste and fitness level. On the Maryland side of the Potomac River is the towpath for the Chesapeake & Ohio Canal; the trail is wide, flat and mostly dirt; on the Virginia side goes the *Appalachian Trail*.

Beside the canal, the Maryland Heights rise dramatically 1,448 feet above the rivers. The *Stone Fort Trail* up the Heights is the park's most strenuous hike and one of the most historic. With the outbreak of the Civil War, the Union

Army sought to fortify the strategic Maryland Heights with its commanding views of the waters and busy railroad lines below. The roads leading to the summit were remembered by Union soldiers as "very rocky, steep and crooked and barely wide enough for those wagons."

Wayside exhibits help canine hikers appreciate the effort involved in dragging guns, mortar and cannon up the mountainside. One 9-inch Dahlgren gun capable of lobbing 100-pound shells weighed 9,700 pounds. The trail leads to the remnants of the Stone Fort which straddles the crest of Maryland Heights at its highest elevation.

You walk your dog across the Potomac River bridge - there is open grating that can intimidate skittish dogs - to Lower Town in Harpers Ferry. Here you will find Virginus Island and the ruins of a thriving industrial town that finally succumbed to flooding in 1889. The trails that weave through the ruins are flat and shady and connect to the trails in historic Lower Town, where John Brown barricaded himself in the town's fire engine house and battled Federal troops. Climbing up the steep grade out of Lower Town is a short trail to Jefferson Rock, where Thomas Jefferson recorded his impressions in 1783.

Trail Sense: There are wonderful maps that help diffuse a potentially confusing tri-state area.

Dog Friendliness
Dogs are welcome in Harpers Ferry.

Traffic
There won't be many trail users in Maryland Heights but your dog will need to be well-socialized in Lower Town.

Canine Swimming
There is some access to the Shenandoah River but this outing with your dog will be for walking, not swimming.

Trail Time
You can spend an entire day enjoying Harpers Ferry with your dog.

10
Mount Vernon

The Park

George Washington, an avid fox-hunter, sought to breed a new type of dog to course the terrain around his estate at Mount Vernon. He crossed French hounds from his friend the Marquis de Lafayette, with his own smaller black-and-tan English hounds. Washington listed 30 new "American" foxhounds by name in his journal and hounds currently registered with the American Kennel Club are descended from those originals. The Father of Our Country often favored silly names for his beloved dogs: Drunkard, Tipler, Tipsy.

The Mount Vernon estate was saved in 1853 by Ann Pamela Cunningham who spearheaded one of the oldest national historic preservation organizations in the country. Today Mount Vernon is the most visited private estate in America.

The Walks

George Washington wrote about his plantation on the Potomac River,

Fairfax

Phone Number
- (703) 780-2000

Website
- www.mountvernon.org/index.cfm/

Admission Fee
- Yes

Park Hours
- Seasonal daily hours to 5:00 p.m.

Directions
- Travel east on I-66 to I-495 South (the Beltway). Follow the outer beltway which becomes I-95 North (headed towards Baltimore). Turn off at exit 177B, Route 1 North, marked Alexandria/Mount Vernon. Once on Route 1, make the first right turn, onto Franklin Street. Turn right again at Washington Street, which is marked for Mount Vernon. Washington Street becomes the George Washington Parkway as you leave Alexandria, and Mount Vernon is eight miles south, at the large traffic circle at the end of the Parkway.

"No estate in United America is more pleasantly situated than this." He controlled 8,000 acres here and today your dog can trot across much of the 500 acres that have been preserved. On the grounds are more than 20 outbuildings and 50 acres of gardens for your dog to explore. She may even meet some grazing livestock.

The *Forest Trail* is a short interpretive walk through a wooded area over a ravine and past an old cobble quarry that was used to create roadways, walkways and the main entrance. This little hike features one steep climb and a wide, groomed path for your dog.

Trail Sense: There are maps and interpretive signs to lead you around the estate.

Dog Friendliness

Mount Vernon welcomes dogs on leashes during visitation hours. The gate attendants provide a bowl of water for canine visitors.

Traffic

As you will most likely be poking around the remote corners of the estate, this should not be a problem.

Canine Swimming

None.

Trail Time

An hour or more.

39

II
Riverbend Park

The Park

George Washington incorporated the Patowmack Company in 1784 to build a canal around Great Falls and open the western Ohio lands directly to Potomac River shipping. Work on the canal began in 1785 and Conn's Ferry was established above the Falls at the site of the present Riverbend Park.

In 1814 President James Madison and his wife Dolley, fleeing the British and the burning of Washington, travelled over the rolling road to Conn's Ferry and escaped into Maryland.

In 1974 Fairfax County established Riverbend Park to preserve 409 acres of mixed hardwoods, a large meadow and a river floodplain. The park features over two miles of frontage on the Potomac River.

Fairfax

Phone Number
- (703) 759-9018

Website
- www.fairfaxcounty.gov/parks/riverbend/

Admission Fee
- None

Park Hours
- 7:00 a.m. to dusk

Directions
- Take Beltway Exit 44 onto Route 193 West (Georgetown Pike) to River Bend Road. Turn right and right again on Jeffery Road and follow for approximately one mile to the park entrance.

The Walks

More than 10 miles of natural-surfaced trail spread out from the Visitors Center and the Nature Center in Riverbend Park. The two centers are only about 1/2-mile apart so you can start your explorations at either place without skipping one. Just about any hike you want to do with your dog is on the menu here: a long multi-hour trek or a short, invigorating loop; a hike in the shade of a mature hardwood forest or an open-air ramble through old fields and emerging trees.

The long-distance *Potomac Heritage Trail* traces - appropriately - the bend in the Potomac River as it travels through the floodplain in the park. The best bet for your dog here (no bikes or horses) is the green-blazed *Paw Paw Passage*

40

Trail (that is the tree, not a dogs-only trail) that departs the back of the Nature Center and rolls down to the Potomac River, passing through a variety of habitats. This sporty loop covers just over one mile.

Trail Sense: There is a trailmap available and the major trails are blazed. Adventurous canine hikers can also take advantage of numerous unmarked dirt trails that criss-cross the park. Squeezed between the river and housing developments you probably won't require a St. Bernard-led rescue party.

Dog Friendliness
Dogs are allowed on the Riverbend Park trails.

Traffic
Bikes and horses are allowed on most park trails but not the two that leave from the Nature Center.

Canine Swimming
The Potomac River is tame enough at this point for your dog to enjoy a swim.

Trail Time
Anywhere from a half-hour loop hike to a full day.

"Dog. A kind of additional or subsidiary Deity designed to catch the overflow and surplus of the world's worship."
-Ambrose Bierce

12
G. Richard Thompson Wildlife Refuge

The Park
The major portion of the management area's two parcels, totaling nearly 4,000 acres, are located in Northwestern Fauquier County. Beginning at its lower reaches, the property rises in a series of steep inclines and benches to the crest of the Blue Ridge. The property's long northwestern boundary closely follows the mountain crest, occasionally straying westward into Warren and Clarke Counties. Elevations range from 700 to 2200 feet.

Though predominantly a hardwood forest, there is some open land at the lower elevations and at the top of the Davenport Tract. Terraced slopes on the lower portion of the area mark where rows of fruit trees once grew. Other physical features of the area include numerous rock outcroppings, and several major streams and ecologically unique spring seeps.

Parking is provided in 11 designated parking lots; two on the eastern slopes along Route 688.

Fauquier

Phone Number
- None

Website
- www.dgif.state.va.us/hunting/wma/thompson.html

Admission Fee
- None

Park Hours
- Dawn to dusk

Directions
- The park is located on the western border of the county off Route 688, north from I-66 or south from Route 50.

The Walks
Trails from both parking lots lead up to the *Appalachian Trail* although the most popular route is from the northern lot at Lake Thompson. This is not a mountain hike with stunning views, dramatic waterfalls or tumbling streams. You'll actually get none of those. But if you are looking for a long walk in the woods with your dog, Thompson Wildlife Refuge is your destination.

The climb to the Appalachian Trail is moderately strenuous and the full loop will cover about eight miles. The Appalachian Trail crosses the park for seven miles. Abandoned homesites and the occasional apple trees from long-ago orchards provide a bit of diversity.

Trail Sense: A trailmap is posted on the information board in the parking lots but you don't want to head off without a map in hand that can be printed off the Internet.

Dog Friendliness

Dogs are allowed on the refuge's mountain trails.

Traffic

This is one of the game department's most popular properties but not nearly as popular as its neighbor to the north, Sky Meadows.

Canine Swimming

The 10-acre Lake Thompson is the best canine swimming hole in Northern Virginia but don't bother the trout fishermen.

Trail Time

A half a day to multi-day adventures on the Appalachian Trail.

13
Scotts Run
Nature Preserve

The Park

Scotts Run Nature Preserve is one that survived. It's not easy to halt the march of progress and like so much of its neighboring land this 340-acre tract of woodland known as the Burling Tract was slated to support a 300-home subdivision in 1970.

Local residents, most prominently Elizabeth Miles Cooke, an artist and historian who lived in a 200-year old house near Swink's Mill Road and Georgetown Pike opposite the current park, fought the planned development bitterly. In a region where the scorecard clearly favored the developers this one went into the win column for the conservationists.

Betty Cooke died in May 1999 at the age of 91 and the bridge that spans Scotts Run not far from her home was named after her.

Fairfax

Phone Number
- None

Website
- None

Admission Fee
- None

Park Hours
- None

Directions
- From the Beltway take Exit 44 onto Route 193 West (Georgetown Pike). The smaller of two parking lots is almost immediately on your right. The main lot is a bit further down on the right.

The Walks

Setting out from the parking lot, the trail system in Scotts Run Nature Preserve pushes towards the Potomac River, either to rocky bluffs above the water or down to the shoreline itself. The journey will take you past shady hemlocks and stately hardwoods on wide, dirt paths (with an occasional stony road thrown in).

Most of this is easy going for your dog (Fairfax County has erected wooden stairs where the climbs start to look daunting) save for the trip to the water's edge that travels on a rocky road. At the time of this writing a large downed tree at the base of the waterfall where Scotts Run plops into the Potomac not

only hindered views but prevented access for your dog for swimming in the plunge pool. A full loop of the preserve can be crafted to cover about a two-mile canine hike but many secondary trails can lengthen your stay.

Trail Sense: There is a trail map posted on the information board at the parking lots but it doesn't begin to identify all the trails in the park. The trails are not marked but "You Are Here" map posts show up at random trail junctions and are always welcomed. Bounded by a major river, a superhighway, a busy commuter cattle chute and a housing subdivision you may get misdirected but hardly lost.

Dog Friendliness
Dogs are permitted in Scotts Run Nature Preserve.

Traffic
Bikes are not allowed on the these trails that are popular with joggers and canine hikers.

Canine Swimming
There are pools in Scotts Run above the waterfall and the edge of the Potomac out of the rapids is suitable for splashing in typical times of low water.

Trail Time
Available for a quick hike or more than one hour.

14
Ellanor C. Lawrence Park

The Park

The first land patents in what is now western Fairfax County were issued in 1727. In that year, Francis Aubrey acquired the land now within the park south of Big Rocky Run. For the next 250 years the property known as Walney belonged to only three families who farmed tobacco, grew grain and raised livestock.

Ellanor Campbell Lawrence, a native of South Carolina, moved to Washington, D.C. in 1916. She met and married David Lawrence, who would later found and publish *U.S. News and World Report*. The Lawrences used Walney as a country estate where Ellanor would landscape and garden.

After her death in 1969, David Lawrence donated 640 acres of land in her memory to be preserved in a natural state.

The Walks

Lawrence Park is not a place where you'll strap a pack onto the back of your dog but there is great variety in its four miles of trails. From the Walney pond lot you can take your dog through a field pond environment and across the street at Cabell's your dog can hike briefly on groomed meadow trails. The *Big Rocky Run Trail* begins its two-mile one-way jaunt through mature woodlands here.

The star hike in Lawrence Park is the *North Loop* that begins in the back of the Walney Visitor Center. For about one mile this natural, paw-friendly path spreads across a mixed forest. In the stream cuts and ravines large hardwoods that were never cleared for cropland can be found while pines and cedars domi-

46

nate in the flatlands as they reclaim the cultivated fields. Your dog certainly won't object to extending this genial canine hike by tacking on another half-mile down the *Wild Turkey Loop*.

Trail Sense: A trailmap is available and out on the property the trails are blazed and distance signs are posted at junctions.

Dog Friendliness
Dogs are welcome on the park trails.

Traffic
Bicycles are permitted on Walney Road and Big Rocky Run Stream Valley Trails but not on the trails around the Walney Visitor Center.

Canine Swimming
None.

Trail Time
More than one hour.

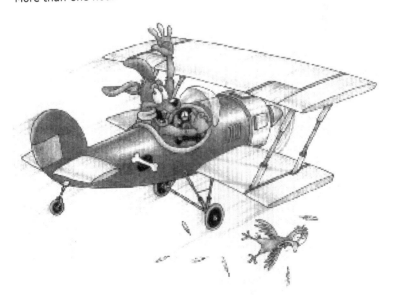

15
Theodore Roosevelt Island

The Park

During his presidency, Theodore Roosevelt set aside over 234 million acres of public lands as national parks, forests, monuments and wildlife refuges. After his death in 1919, Roosevelt admirers sought a suitable memorial - and what better way to honor his legacy of conservation than by dedicating this wooded, 88-acre island in the Potomac River in his memory?

In Colonial times the island was a summer resort for wealthy Virginians; the Mason family owned it for 125 years. In the early 1800's, John Mason built a brick mansion and cultivated extensive gardens but abandoned the property in 1832 when a causeway built across the river stagnated his water.

A hundred years later the Theodore Roosevelt Memorial Association purchased the island. Congress approved funds in 1960 and the memorial was dedicated on October 27, 1967.

Arlington

Phone Number
- (703) 289-2500

Website
- www.nps.gov/this/

Admission Fee
- None

Park Hours
- Dawn to Dusk

Directions
- Theodore Roosevelt Island is accessible by foot from a parking lot off the northbound lanes of the George Washington Memorial Parkway. Traveling southbound, take Theodore Roosevelt Bridge to Constitution Ave. Take a right on 23rd Street and cross Memorial Bridge. Once on the bridge, bear right to return to the Parkway.

The Walks

Three curvilinear trails conspire to cover the marsh, swamp and forest of the island. The *Upland Trail* and *Wood Trail* are covered with imbedded yellow stones; the *Swamp Trail* utilizes a boardwalk. All are extremely wide and ideal when more than one dog is in tow. There is enough elevation change to keep your interest and the thick woods produce a shady haven just yards from the crush of Washington bustle. Of course the speeding auto traffic and overhead

flights from Reagan National Airport are sure to get your dog's attention.

Trail Sense: There is a map on the bulletin board at the footbridge and you may be lucky enough to catch a brochure but if not the trails run lengthwise along the island.

Dog Friendliness

Dogs are welcome on the island - Roosevelt, whose family was famous for the pets it kept in the White House - would have it no other way.

Traffic

There is limited parking at the site and most of those are cyclists using the *Mount Vernon Trail* - bikes are not permitted on the island.

Canine Swimming

Your dog can slip into the Potomac River for a dip in places, at the footbridge where it reaches the island, for one.

Trail Time

You can spend upwards of an hour exploring the island with your dog. Parking in the lot is limited to two hours to discourage commuters.

16
Banshee Reeks Nature Preserve

The Park

Legend has it that an early landowner of these rolling hills was of Irish or Scottish descent. After a night of revelry in a nearby town he returned to his farm and heard what he thought were "banshees in the reeks" - translated from Gaelic as female spirits in the hills. When the 695-acre passive nature park was established the name of local lore was given to the preserve.

The land was acquired by Loudoun County in 1995 and envisioned as a typical active recreation park of picnic sites and ballfields. But public agitation led to the establishment of the preserve, believed to be one of the few nature preserves of this scale operated by a county government in the country.

The Walks

Banshee Reeks was originally developed for use by organized groups but has been opened to the general public one weekend per month. Call ahead to determine if any restrictions are in effect. Canine hikers will want to make the special effort required to use these trails.

Paw-friendly grass trails are cut through the stunning meadows and well-maintained trails traipse through riparian forests. Expect stream crossings and a good workout for you and your dog. Pay attention to avoid trails that are closed for maintenance or under construction so that public access will not be

Loudoun

Phone Number
- (703) 669-0316

Website
- www.co.loudoun.va.us/prcs/parks/banshee.htm

Admission Fee
- None

Park Hours
- 8:00 a.m. to 4:00 p.m. on the third Saturday and Sunday of each month

Directions
- Take U.S. Route 15 South from Leesburg. Approximately 1/4-mile South of the Leesburg Bypass, turn left onto Route 621, Evergreen Mills Road. Proceed south along Evergreen Mills Road about five miles. Turn right onto The Woods Road (Route 771). Proceed down The Woods Road (a dirt road) for approximately one mile. Entrance to Banshee Reeks is on the left.

closed for maintenance or under construction so that public access will not be restricted.

Trail Sense: A trailmap is available and the paths are named and marked.

Dog Friendliness
Dogs are allowed on Banshee trails.
Traffic
Foot traffic only.
Canine Swimming
The trails touch on Goose Creek in several spots.
Trail Time
Several hours are available.

"They are superior to human beings as companions.
They do not quarrel or argue with you.
They never talk about themselves but listen to you while you
talk about yourself, and keep an appearance of being interested
in the conversation."
                                                    -Jerome K. Jerome

17
Accotink Bay
Wildlife Refuge

The Park

Accotink Bay Wildlife Refuge is a nature preserve on the grounds of Fort Belvoir. The refuge was established in 1979 to protect sensitive wetlands and wildlife habitats associated with Accotink Bay and to provide opportunities for environmental education and low-intensity recreation.

In 1988, Fort Belvoir established a second refuge, the Jackson Miles Abbott Wetland Refuge, to protect another sensitive wetland area and to provide opportunities for wildlife watching. Abbott was an army engineer whose ornithological illustrations were chosen to appear on a duck stamp.

Today, more than one-third of the installation's acreage has been preserved as a designated wildlife sanctuary encompassing over 1,300 acres.

The Walks

There are some fifteen short, intersecting trail segments on both sides of the Accotink Creek to explore with your dog here. The going can be a bit rough at times, especially along the creek where the narrow bands of pathway can be overgrown or muddy in wet tmes but overall this is easy going with some mild ups and downs.

The highlight ramble in the refuge is the *Beaver Pond Trail* loop that

Fairfax

Phone Number
- (703) 806-4007

Website
- www.dgif.state.va.us/wildlife/vbwt/site.asp?trail=1&site=CMN05&loop=CMN

Admission Fee
- None

Hours
- Dawn to dusk

Directions
- The refuge is located on the Fort Belvoir Military Base. From I-95 take the Fort Belvoir/Newington exit to the southern leg of the Fairfax County Parkway (Route 7100). Follow the parkway east approximately 3 miles until its end at Richmond Highway (Route 1). Turn left onto Route 1 and at the first light make a right into Tulley Gate. Follow to the refuge main entrance ahead on the right. Before that, the first parking lot you see is for the short handicap accessible trail; the second leads to the heart of the trail system. Access to the base, of course, can be limited without notice.

slips past several small ponds filled with turtles and frogs. For a longer leg stretcher head down the *Great Blue Heron Trail* to a bird blind on the Accotink Bay.

Across the suspension bridge are miles of dirt trails in the hardwood forest that was once used for target ranges. The Abbott Wetland Refuge has a one-mile asphalt trail with an observation deck overlooking the wetland area.

Trail Sense: There are signs at trail junctions and mapboards in the parking lots. Another mapboard is judiciously placed at the suspension bridge in the middle of the trail system to reinforce any canine hiking plans.

Dog Friendliness
Dogs are permitted on the trails in the refuge.
Traffic
Foot traffic only and not much of it.
Canine Swimming
The Accotink Creek is deep enough for a fine doggie swim and there is a wide, pebbly shoreline for easy access to the water.
Trail Time
More than one hour.

18
Whitney
State Forest

The Park

The Commonwealth uses this 147-acre forest for timber production and research. Whitney State Forest is a designated wildlife sanctuary. There are no facilities or amenities on the property.

The Walks

This off-the-beaten-path woodland serves up almost six miles of trails for your dog to enjoy. An old fire road runs through most of the property but you will want to slip off onto the extensive network of narrow dirt paths. Come with a mind to explore because you won't get any wayfinding aids in Whitney State Forest.

This is mostly hardwood but you'll likely stumble on a surprise or two in this airy forest, like a grove of loblolly pines. The terrain can get downright hilly depending on the route you choose and you can get your dog quite a workout here.

Trail Sense: You are on your own in Whitney State Forest but you can use the fire road for orientation.

Fauquier

Phone Number
- None

Website
- www.dgif.state.va.us/wildlife/vbwt/site.asp?trail=3&site=PCU04&loop=PCU

Admission Fee
- None

Park Hours
- 7:00 a.m - 7:00 p.m.

Directions
- The forest is south of Warrenton. From the James Madison Highway make a right onto Lovers Lane (Route 744). Continue to the T-intersection at the end. Make a left onto Lees Ridge Road (Route 684) to the forest parking lot on the right.

Dog Friendliness
Dogs are allowed through-out Whitney State Forest.

Traffic
The park is open to foot traffic only - no vehicles.

Canine Swimming
None.

Trail Time
Up to half a day.

19
Potomac Overlook Regional Park

The Park
This property was owned by the Mason family until 1842 when Robert Donaldson purchased 98 acres for a farm. Donaldson operated a market farming enterprise, taking his produce of grain, vegetables and fruit to sell across the river in Georgetown. Several members of the Donaldson family continued to reside on the property into the 20th century.

Unlike similar neighboring parks Potomac Overlook is not the result of any fervent conservation movement. In 1942, a developer, in fact, purchased 35 acres to build a residential community but couldn't sell any homesites.

The land was never developed and was eventually purchased by NVRPA in 1966 and the wedge of woodland adjacent to the George Washington Parkway was developed into a 67-acre park with assistance from the National Audubon Society.

Arlington

Phone Number
- (703) 528-5406

Website
- www.nvrpa.org/potomacover-look.html

Admission Fee
- None

Hours
- Daylight hours

Directions
- Take I-66 to the Spout Run exit. Turn left on Lee Highway, right on Military Road and right on Marcey Road, which deadends at the park.

The Walks
Canine hiking is unfailingly pleasant in this park dominated by woodland. Your dog will find well-maintained, airy paths that roll easily around the property. There are some two miles of marked and named trails in Potomac Overlook Regional park but you are seldom more than ten minutes from the Nature Center at the center of the property.

The trails are peppered with massive tulip poplars and oaks and the green-blazed *Heritage Trail* scoots through a heritage orchard from the early 1900s. Tucked into the woods are many reminders of human habitation - house foundations, a spring house, a cemetery. You can also visit various gardens with your dog.

Park trails link to several nearby trails outside the park including the *Donaldson Run Trail* that works down the ridge to the *Potomac River Heritage Trail*. You can transition from a leisurely stroll to an ardent hike with your dog with this option.

Trail Sense: A trailmap, information board, blazes and signage are all available to keep you on track.

Dog Friendliness
Dogs can enjoy these wonderful trails.
Traffic
Bikes are not allowed on the trail.
Canine Swimming
Streams in the park are more suitable for minnows to swim in than dogs.
Trail Time
An hour or more is possible.

20
Red Rock Wilderness Regional Park

The Park

This longtime farm on the palisades of the Upper Potomac River was purchased as a parkland with the help of Mrs. Frances Speck, who donated half the value of the property. The farmland has regenerated into woodlands that completely cover the 67-acre park.

The Walks

When you set out into the woods behind the parking lot there is no way for your dog to guess at the workout that awaits her. The birch and oak trees here are almost completely devoid of any understory and there is plenty of elbow room for a whole pack of dogs if need be.

Loudoun

Phone Number
- (703) 737-7800

Website
- www.nvrpa.org/redrock.html

Admission Fee
- None

Park Hours
- Dawn to dusk

Directions
- Take Route 7 West toward Leesburg and take the Route 15 Bypass North. Turn right on Edwards Ferry Road (Route 773) and drive 1.5 miles to the park entrance on the left.

After a few easy steps a little hook trail detours down to the Potomac River floodplain for more easy hiking with your dog. Once back atop the bluff the trail begins to dip and turn in and out of two ravines before you reach the namesake overlook after about one mile. It is another half-mile back to the parking lot but the forest has changed completely, congested with cedars and pin oaks. The trail is narrower but the terrain is flat again.

Several connector trails are available for additional time with your dog in this quiet woodland.

Trail Sense: Trail maps are available at the trailhead. It has been awhile since the paths were blazed - they grow fainter with each visit.

Dog Friendliness
Dogs are free to test the trails in Red Rock Wilderness.
Traffic
Bicycles and motorized vehicles are prohibited on trails. Don't expect much competition for the trails.
Canine Swimming
There is easy access to the Potomac River when it is not too wet.
Trail Time
About one hour.

21
Turkey Run Park

The Park

Turkey Run provided fine hunting and fishing grounds for American Indians who lived here for thousands of years until the 1700s. Among the early Colonial owners of the land which now includes Turkey Run Park was Lighthorse Harry Lee, father of Robert E. Lee.

The Reid family acquired control of most of this land around 1820, raising corn and wheat for the next 80 years. Their farmstead was onproperty that now houses the CIA Headquarters, adjacent to Turkey Run Park. A grist mill no longer visible operated just north of Turkey Run stream.

The nature of Turkey Run was altered dramatically during the Civil War, Union troops occupied this area at Fort Marcy, one of 67 forts that circled Washington D.C. during the hostilities. Every tree around Turkey Run was chopped down to ward off sneak attacks.

Fairfax

Phone Number
- (703)289-2500

Website
- www.nps.gov/archive/gwmp/vapa/turkey.htm

Admission Fee
- None

Park Hours
- Sunrise to sunset

Directions
- From Beltway Exit 14, follow the George Washington Memorial Parkway two miles to the Turkey Run Park exit on the right. Follow signs into the park. From Washington, D.C. and Old Town Alexandria: take the GWMP north approximately eight miles and exit right at the Turkey Run Park sign. Make the first right turn into the park. Turkey Run is accessible only from the parkway.

Before acquired by the National Park Service a dairy farm operated here until the 1930s. Now it serves primarily as a picnic park.

The Walks

The *Turkey Hill Loop Trail* is as hilly a workout as you can give your dog in the Northern Virginia suburbs. Rock steps and switchbacks are used to get you down to the bottom of a rugged little gorge take takes Turkey Run to the

Potomac River. At the bottom of the palisades you can hook into the _Potomac Heritage Trail_ that runs ten miles from Theodore Roosevelt Island to the American Legion Bridge. The hike to the American Legion Bridge from this point is a little more than 1.5 miles. Turkey Run cuts just one of twelve ravines in the park and it features water year-round.

Back atop the 200-foot bluffs the _Woods Trail_ rolls among all three picnic areas. The trees on the rocky hillsides have recovered so successfully since the Civil war that the hardwood forest - studded with beech and oak and hickory - is considered one of the finest hardwood forests in Northern Virginia.

Trail Sense: The information board at the trailhead features brochures and a posted trail map. The trails are also blazed.

Dog Friendliness
Dogs are welcome on the trails and in the picnic areas.
Traffic
Bikes are not allowed on the trails.
Canine Swimming
Yes, at the edge of the Potomac River.
Trail Time
About one hour.

"The greatest pleasure of a dog is that you may make a fool of yourself with him, and not only will he not scold you, but will make a fool of himself too."
- Samuel Butler

22
C.M. Crockett
Park

The Park

Twelve German families migrated to this area in 1719 to mine ore on 1,805 acres on Licking Run. They were the first Europeans to establish a permanent settlement in what is now Fauquier County and created the first German reformed congregation in the Southern colonies.

The town survived into the 20th century but was abandoned by World War II. No trace of the town remains today and the quarry from which they extracted ore has been filled in to create 109-acre Germantown Lake

The Walks

There are two main hiking routes to enjoy with your dog on opposite ends of the park. Each offers a bit over a mile of easy going on maintained trails.

Fauquier

Phone Number
- (540) 788-4867

Website
- www.fauquiercounty.gov/government/departments/parksrec/index.cfm?action=crockett

Admission Fee
- $6.00 for non-county folks

Park Hours
- 7:00 a.m. to dusk, March through October; 9:00 a.m.-5:00 p.m. November through February

Directions
- Crockett Park is south of Warrenton on Route 643 (Meetze Road), just north of Route 28.

The *Bluebird Cross Country Trail* takes in the open fields above the lake before dropping into the trees at the shoreline, crossing the dam and looping around the spillway. A mature woodland awaits across the picnic area on the *Four Seasons Nature Trail*, a series of three stacked loops. Your dog will find this ramble to be exceedingly paw-friendly and don't be surprised if he wants to go around again.

Trail Sense: The trails are marked and a trailmap is available.

Dog Friendliness

Dogs are welcome in Crockett Park.

Traffic

The Picnic Area Loop can support wheeled vehicles but not the natural surface trails. You have to walk to all the activity areas and that does keep some folks from reaching them.

Canine Swimming

There is no swimming in the lake for people or dogs.

Trail Time

More than one hour.

23
Huntley Meadows Park

The Park

In 1905, a year after arriving in New York City, 21-year old Mario Casalegno of Turin, Italy was not living the American dream. He was serving a four-year prison term for killing a fellow employee in a restaurant where he worked as a cook.

Two decades later, when he arrived at this Hybla Valley land that had once been in the Geroge Mason family for over 100 years, Casalegno - now known as Henry Woodhouse - had been the leading aviation writer in America, involved in Turkish oil dealings, worked on the fringes of Hollywood and was a leading collector of memorabilia connected to George Washington.

Woodhouse's vision was to create the world's largest airport with a 7200- foot runway and mooring fields for trans-Atlantic Zeppelin fleets. At the gates of the national capital, the airfield would also contain a shrine to George Washington. During 1929 he acquired over 1,500 acres of land from ten landowners but by 1935 all the land was in forecloseure and purchased by the federal government. In 1975, five years after the colorful Woodhouse died with some 35 lawsuits still pending against him, President Gerald Ford donated the land to the citizens of Fairfax County for exclusive use as a public park.

Fairfax

Phone Number
- (703) 768-2525

Website
- www.fairfaxcounty.gov/ parks/huntley/

Admission Fee
- None

Park Hours
- Dawn to Dusk

Directions
- Take Beltway Exit 1 (Richmond Highway, Route 1) and go south 3.5 miles. Make a right on Lockheed Boulevard to the park entrance in .5 miles on the left where the road makes a 90-degree right turn.

The Walks

The 1,424 acres of Huntley Meadows Park is one of the finest natural areas in the shadow of Washington D.C. - although not for dog owners. Dogs are allowed in the park and you can get an exceedingly pleasant, easy-going canine hike here but dogs are not allowed on the 1/2-mile boardwalk of the *Heron Trail* that leads into the cattail-studded freshwater marsh.

The main dog-hiking route is on the *Cedar Trail/Deer Trail* leading away from the Visitor Center for about one mile. If you are enjoying the level grounds and shady woods consider the *Informal Trail* off the Deer Trail. This is a narrow band that is not maintained and best left alone when wet but is largely unused and a good place to wander off with your dog. Other options for canine hiking here include a path adjacent to the parking lot that leaves the park to the Huntley Manor House and the 1.2-mile linear *Hike-Bike Trail* that can be accessed from a parking lot on South Kings Highway.

Trail Sense: There are excellent maps posted on bulletin boards and in the park brochure. If that is not enough there are markers along the trails that let you know exactly where you are.

Dog Friendliness
Dogs are allowed on the park trails but cannot go on the boardwalk so you can't complete a loop.
Traffic
These wide trails are popular with walkers and wildlife watchers. The crushed stone main trails also support strollers. Bikes are permitted only on the remote Hike/Bike Trail.
Canine Swimming
None.
Trail Time
You can spend over an hour hiking with your dog here.

"If there are no dogs in Heaven, then when I die
I want to go where they went."
-anonymous

24
Conway-Robinson State Forest

The Park

This swath of 444 acres of Prince William County open space provides outdoor recreation opportunities and protects water quality conditions in the Occoquan watershed.

There are no facilities or amenities in the park, save for a few scattered picnic tables.

The Walks

The trail system in the Conway-Robinson State Forest is a perimeter loop embracing a series of stacked loops. Your canine hike begins as a common woods walk but you shortly cross a pipeline cut and enter an area known as The Pines - as lovely a stretch of path as you are likely to find in the region.

Prince William

Phone Number
- None

Website
- www.dgif.state.va.us/wildlife/vbwt/site.asp?trail=3&site=PCU02&loop=PCU

Admission Fee
- None

Park Hours
- Dawn to Dusk

Directions
- There are no signs for the forest that is on the north side of the Lee Highway (Route 29) sandwiched between Manassas National Battlefield and I-66. Look for a small picnic area.

Most of the forest is on level ground - save this outing for a dry day since the ground can get wet - although it slopes a bit after the pipeline. The trail narrows again after the pine trees as you move into a typical oak-hickory forest. The trail often winds back on itself to give it the feel of a greater length than its two miles.

Trail Sense: There is a trailmap posted on the information board at the trailhead but out in the trees the trails are sporadically marked.

Dog Friendliness

Dogs are allowed on these trails.

Traffic

Most of the traffic will be of the two-wheeled variety.

Canine Swimming

None.

Trail Time

About an hour.

25
Mason Neck National Wildlife Refuge

The Park

George Mason, the brilliant mind behind the Virginia Bill of Rights, predecessor to the United States Bill of Rights, came to this wooded peninsula in 1775. He built a magnificent Georgian mansion he called Gunston Hall, which was his home until his death in 1792.

Over the next 100 years the 8,000-acre peninsula was heavily logged until most of the mature pine and hardwoods were completely gone. By the 1960s residential development posed a threat to the regenerating forest and the local bald eagle population.

In 1969 more than 6,000 acres were dedicated by the U.S. Fish & Wildlife Service as the first national wildlife refuge specifically established for the bald eagle.

Fairfax

Phone Number
- (703) 490-4979

Website
- www.fws.gov/refuges/profiles/index.cfm?id=51610

Admission Fee
- None

Hours
- 8:00 a.m. to sunset

Directions
- From I-95 exit into Lorton on Route 642 East. Turn right on Route 1 (Richmond Highway) and left on Route 242 (Gunston Road). Continue on Route 600 past Gunston Plantation, making a right onto High Point Road at the sign for Mason Neck State Park/National Refuge and follow to park.

The Walks

There are a few options for you and your dog to explore this quiet sanctuary with more than four miles of shoreline. The marquee hike in Mason Neck NWR is the *Woodmarsh Trail* - flat, wide and leafy. This balloon-shaped trail takes you to the fringes of the Great Marsh and an observation tower. This is the largest freshwater marsh in northern Virginia and home to the finest Great Blue heron rookery in the Mid-Atlantic region. A round trip on the Woodmarsh Trail will cover about three miles.

If you want to spend extra time in these airy, hickory-and-oak woods you can set off with your dog down one of the refuge roads that are closed to the

public or drive to the other side of the refuge and take the paved, 3/4-mile *Great Marsh Trail* down to another observation tower.

Trail Sense: The refuge features all the standard wayfinding aids - trail map, blazes and junction signs but they don't completely coordinate. It is a good idea to jot down notes from the mapboard in the parking lot to clarify what you'll find in the brochure and out on the trail when portions are closed for nesting.

Dog Friendliness
Dogs are welcome in the refuge.
Traffic
Very little; the trails are for foot traffic only; bikes are allowed only on the paved *High Point Multi-Use Trail* that runs the length of the peninsula.
Canine Swimming
None.
Trail Time
More than one hour.

26

Mason District Park

The Park

This land was first cultivated in 1650 as part of William Fitzhugh's mammoth Ravensworth Plantation. Ravensworth was the largest single parcel of land granted in Northern Virginia. This area began to be subdivided after 1797 and in 1808 - the same year the Columbia Pike opened - Aspen Hill Farm began. The soil started to give out before the Civil War and from 1870 to 1970 these hills supported a pony farm.

The county acquired the land for a park in the 1970s but the park was slow to develop. In 1980 a local jogger trying to slog along the trails discovered that the staff lacked even a weed-whacker to maintain the park. Civic-minded volunteers organized the Friends of Mason District Park and staged the first park festival as a fundraiser in October 1980. Enough money was raised not only for a weed whacker but also a tractor.

Today's 121-acre park is blend of recreational activities and a managed conservation area.

Fairfax

Phone Number
- (703) 941-1730

Website
- www.fairfaxcounty.gov/parks/omp.htm#23

Admission Fee
- None

Park Hours
- Daylight hours

Directions
- In Annandale, take Exit 52B from the Beltway onto Route 236 East. two miles to a left on John Marr Drive. Turn right on Columbia Pike to park entrance on the right just before Sleepy Hollow Road.

The Walks

The trail system leaves along Turkeycock Run on the shady *Forest Trail* that climbs into the back of the park on stony roads and dirt paths. A quick detour can be taken onto the quarter-mile *Meadow Trail* on wide grass paths. Both eventually reach the Meadowview Shelter for views.

Maybe the best canine hike in Mason District Park is the trek to the dog park next to the Columbia Elementary School. It is about a half-mile on roomy, paw-friendly paths to reach the large, natural-surfaced fenced enclosure (capacity: 62 dogs).

Trail Sense: There is a trail map available but markings on the trail are few and far between. The route to the dog park is well-signed and marked by white paint.

Dog Friendliness
Dogs are allowed in the park and an off-leash dog park is on site.
Traffic
This is a busy park although the trails are less used than the recreation area. Bikes are allowed on the trails.
Canine Swimming
Turkeycock Run is not suitable for a swim.
Trail Time
You can spend about an hour in the Mason District Park woods.

"Happiness is dog-shaped."
-Chapman Pincher

27
Bull Run-Occoquan Trail

The Park

The word "Occoquan" is roughly translated from the Doag Indians of the Powhatan Confederacy who originally inhabited the stream valley, using it as a wilderness highway. With European settlement the indigenous peoples moved away and not much happened until the arrival of the Orange and Alexandria Railroad in 1848.

When the Civil War erupted the first clash between the North and South took place on the south bank of Bull Run. The Bull Run/Occoquan River comprised the boundary of the "Alexandria Line" set up by the Confederates to protect against a Union move towards the capital in Richmond. The town of Clifton was the southernmost post for the Union.

When the war ended Clifton enjoyed a brief flurry of prosperity as the home to the healing waters of Paradise Springs where several presidents reportedly came to take the cure. Clifton was the first town in Fairfax County to be electrified. After the county acquired over 5,000 acres of land along the rivers it created a series of parks cnnected by the *Bull Run-Occoquan Trail*.

Fairfax
Phone Number - None
Website - None
Admission Fee - None
Hours - Dawn to dusk
Directions - Access in various parks

The Walks

If you have a car shuttle this could be the best place to hike with your dog in northern Virginia. The 18-mile trail begins in the east in Fountainhead Regional Park and by the time you reach Bull Run Regional Park your dog will experience most of what the region has to offer.

Hills and stream valleys predominate from Fountainhead to Bull Run Marina, a distance of about 6.5 miles. On the trail to Hemlock Regional Park stands of dark green Eastern hemlocks begin to mix into the forest with the tall beeches and oaks. When the trail reaches Bull Run it begins to level out and hug the shoreline. You'll emerge from the woods more often and the trail can even get muddy and downright impassable in wet weather. An access point where Route 28 crosses Bull Run slices the western segment of the trail into manageable hiking chunks (on the Fairfax side of the stream take the last driveway on the right before crossing the bridge).

Trail Sense: The route is mapped and well-marked with blue blazes throughout.

Dog Friendliness

Dogs can hike the length of the Bull Run-Occoquan Trail and are welcome in all the parks it passes through.

Traffic

Bikes are not allowed on the trail but horses can use it.

Canine Swimming

The side streams are mostly deep enough just for splashing but Bull Run can pool deep enough in spots for a doggie dip.

Trail Time

Anything up to an entire day.

28
Julie J. Metz Wetlands Mitigation Bank

The Park

The Julie J. Metz. Wetlands Bank is the first wetlands bank in Northern Virginia approved by the U.S. Corps of Engineers. A mitigation bank is an area of constructed, restored or preserved wetlands that are important to filter run-off, prevent erosion, improve water quality and provide habitat for wildlife.

Construction began in 1995 and the final grades were completed in 1997. The wetland preserve is named for Julie Metz, an environmental engineer with the Corps of Engineers who fell victim to breast cancer in 1995 at the age of 38.

The 227-acre wetland preserve was donated to the Prince William County for ongoing care and maintenance.

Fairfax
Phone Number - None
Website - None
Admission Fee - None
Park Hours - Dawn to dusk
Directions - Take Route 1 to Neabsco Road in Woodbridge. Turn left into the wetlands bank parking lot just past Leesylvania Elementary School.

The Walks

This is a rare chance in Northern Virginia for your dog to explore a wetlands environment. There are some two miles of level, easy-hiking paths cut into a mosaic around the various pods of the mostly dry marsh. The surface alternates between wood chips, grass and boardwalk - all paw-friendly.

Views are limited in the high marsh grasses that give way to shrubs and scrub forests. The main route is along a 12-station interpretive trail (go left out of the parking lot to pick it up in the designed order.

Trail Sense: The trails are not marked but you should have no great problems getting back to the parking lot.

Dog Friendliness
Dogs are allowed on the trails.

Traffic
Foot traffic only; the parking lot is large enough for only a few cars.

Canine Swimming
None.

Trail Time
About one hour.

29
Weston Wildlife Refuge

The Park

The rambling frame building that is now Weston began life as a log cabin around 1810 and is one of the oldest Colonial houses in Fauquier County. Charles Joseph Nourse from Georgetown purchased the property in 1859 and named it for his ancestral home Weston Hall in England.

Following Nourse's death in 1906, his widow, Annie, operated a school and summer camp here. During World War II the Nourse daughters maintained Weston as a hospitality center for servicemen, serving some 11,000 meals by the end of the war.

Weston and its important collection of outbuildings is now a farm museum owned by the Warrenton Antiquarian Society on 10 acres of the 271-acre refuge.

Fauquier

Phone Number
- None

Website
- None

Admission Fee
- None

Park Hours
- Dawn to Dusk

Directions
- The refuge is southeast of Warrenton. From Warrenton take Route 643 East (Meetze Road) to Route 616 (Casanova Road) to the crossroads of Casanova. Pick up Route 747, Weston Road, to the end of the road and Weston. Take a left to the refuge parking area when you spot Weston outbuildings.

The Walks

The canine hiking across the Weston Wildlife Refuge takes place on two stacked loop trails divided by an old woods road that can be used to close the loops. The orange-blazed *Nourse Woods Trail* rambles through an eastern deciduous forest on rough, unmaintained paths but the going is easy enough for any dog.

The *Turkey Run Trail* trips through dense thickets of cedar that have replaced the former farmland. Turkey Run itself has high banks and limited, overgrown access. Be aware that the refuge is open to hunting but it is chase only - no firearms allowed. Primitive camping is also allowed in the refuge.

Trail Sense: There is a trailmap at the information board and the trails are well-marked (they need to be).

Dog Friendliness

Dogs are allowed across the refuge.

Traffic

Horses use the trail down by Turkey Run but don't be surprised if you don't see anyone on your hike.

Canine Swimming

Turkey Run is wide enough for some spirited splashing but not deep enough for a swim.

Trail Time

About one hour.

30
Ball's Bluff
Regional Park

The Park

In the early days of the Civil War both armies centered around the Potomac River. General Charles P. Stone was directed to move the Confederates out of the Leesburg area and ordered a scouting party across the river from his camp in Maryland.

Once across the Potomac haystacks were mistaken for enemy tents which lured the Union men deeper onto Ball's Bluff and attracted the attention of the Confederates. On the morning of October 21, 1861 the Southern soldiers engaged the enemy and drove the Union army back toward the bluff's edge.

At 4:30 p.m. Colonel Edward Baker, a lifelong friend of President Abraham Lincoln, tried to rally the Northerners out of their trapped position. Baker leapt to the front of the line and was mortally wounded by four musket balls. Suddenly emboldened, the Confederates routed the Union soldiers and pushed them to the edge of the 80-foot bluff. Some scrambled down the cliff only to be picked off by Confederate bullets or drowned under the weight of their uniforms and ammunition. Five hundred and fifty-three Union troops, about 1/3 of their force, were captured.

Coming on the heels of the disaster at Bull Run, Ball's Bluff was another embarassing blow to the North. There were reports of dead bodies floating past the city of Washington. Looking for a scapegoat, Congress censored Stone for committing the "most atrocious blunder in history." He was imprisoned and in later battles, Union commanders would fail to act for fear of similar Congressional reprimand.

Loudoun

Phone Number
- (703) 737-7800

Website
- www.nvrpa.org/ballsbluff.html

Admission Fee
- None

Park Hours
- Dawn to Dusk

Directions
- Take Route 7 to Route 15 Bypass North, just east of Leesburg. From Route 15, turn right on Battlefield Parkway and left on Ball's Bluff Road to the parking lot at the end of the road.

The Walks

The centerpiece hike in the 223-acre park is a one-mile interpretive loop that can get steep and rugged in places after a benign start on soft wood chips. The *Old Cart Path* leads down the bluff to the edge of the Potomac River that gives you a feel of what the Union Army had to face to pull two howitzers and a cannon into position on the battlefield - and try to escape under withering enemy fire. There are other unmarked natural trails through the woods on the edge of the Potomac River.

Trail Sense: The park brochure features a trail map and the *Interpretive Trail* is blazed in white.

Dog Friendliness
Dogs are welcome to explore the battlefield.
Traffic
Foot traffic only and it is limited.
Canine Swimming
The Old Cart Path will take your dog to the muddy banks of the Potomac for swim time in the river.
Trail Time
A leisurely hour.

"No one appreciates the very special genius of your
conversation as a dog does."
-Christopher Morley

31
Burke Lake Park

The Park

Silas Burke, a wealthy plantation owner, was a high ranking Fairfax County official who was instrumental in bringing the Orange and Alexandria railroad to the area. A century later, however, there was not a similar celebration when a different mode of transportation wanted to serve the sparsely populated farming community.

In the 1950s the federal government proposed building Dulles Airport in Burke, buying land and condemning property. The handful of local residents opposed the plan so vehemently that the government scuttled its plans and gave the land to the Fairfax County Park Authority who built the 889-acre park with its 218-acre, man-made lake as a centerpiece. A half-century later, instead of jet planes, visitors to Burke find instead a miniature railroad and the quiet hum of the occasional electric motorboat on the lake.

Fairfax

Phone Number
- (703) 323-6600

Website
- www.fairfaxcounty.gov/parks/burkelake/

Admission Fee
- $8.oo for non-county residents on weekends and holidays

Park Hours
- Grounds dawn to dusk

Directions
- From Route 66 take the Fairfax County Parkway, Exit 55A (7100 South towards Springfield). Continue on the Fairfax County Parkway for approximately five miles. Take a right onto Burke Lake Road. At the next light, turn left onto Ox Road (Route 123). The main entrance - past the boaters' lot - is on the right.

The Walks

There is but one trail at Burke Lake - a hard-packed dirt-and-crushed-stone affair that circumnavigates the lake. Once you set out you sign on for the entire 4.5 miles that hug the shoreline around the many fingers of the lake. The going is almost completely level and under trees just about the whole way around. Views of the lake are abundant and once you clear the active recreation area this lakeside canine hike can impart quite a sense of tranquility for such a developed area.

Trail Sense: There are mapboards but as long as you keep the lake on the same side all the way around you will make it back to your start point.

Dog Friendliness
Dogs are welcome to use the *Lake Loop Trail*. Dogs are also permitted in the family campground.

Traffic
This can be a busy trail, especially near the recreation area where many users are sampling the path. The wide, flat path is a magnet for trail runners and scholastic cross-country teams. Bikes are allowed on the trail.

Canine Swimming
Plenty of places to test the water for a doggie dip.

Trail Time
Allow about two hours for a complete circuit of Burke Lake.

32
Bull Run
Regional Park

The Park

The first English settlers in the area called the peripatetic stream Bull Run, the term applied to creeks unaffected by tidal influence and therefore flowed in only one direction. The waterway provided easy transportation and sustenance to those who lived along it and it would have continued forever in anonymity like so many thousands of similar streams if it wasn't by chance a key defensive line between the North and South during the Civil War.

Today the forest on the north shore of Bull Run is left undisturbed as a sanctuary protected by the Northern Virginia Regional Park Authority.

The Walks

The first thing your dog will find when he hangs his head out the window driving into Bull Run Regional Park is

Fairfax

Phone Number
- (703) 631-0550

Website
- www.nvrpa.org/bullrunpark.html

Admission Fee
- Yes, vehicle entrance fee charged to non-member jurisdictions; weekly and annual passes available

Park Hours
- Dawn to dusk, mid-March to November

Directions
- Take I-66 to Exit 52 (Route 29) at Centreville, drive 2 miles south, turn left onto Bull Run Post Office Road and follow the signs to the park entrance.

that he won't need his climbing gear. The next thing is the abundance of large, open fields. You could spend a sunny day just hiking with your dog around these wide open spaces in the 1,500-acre park and never venture onto the trails.

The park is the northern terminus for the *Bull Run-Occoquan Trail* that runs for 18 miles along the water to Fountainhead Park. The segment here scrambles 1.72 miles to a parking lot on Route 28. This and other trails are wide and flat and make for easy canine hiking - and also muddy when wet.

Trail Sense: A trail map is available but not all the park's trails are blazed. The Bull Run-Occoquan Trail is marked in blue.

Dog Friendliness

Dogs are allowed on the trails and in the campground.

Traffic

Bicycles and motorized vehicles are prohibited on all trails. You may encounter a horse or two in the big park.

Canine Swimming

The streams can occasionally flow deep enough to serve as more than a splashpool.

Trail Time

Many hours are possible.

33

Occoquan Regional Park

The Park

In 1910 the federal government purchased land along the picturesque Occoquan River for a new prison. A product of the reform movement of the day, the new Occoquan Workhouse stressed that "a prisoner's hard physical work, learned skills and fresh air would transform him into a model citizen." So the small initial cadre of 60 inmates worked building and maintaining a 1,200-acre farm.

The Workhouse gained national notoriety in 1916 when about 170 women were arrested for their participation in marches in front of the White House on behalf of suffrage and were brought to Occoquan. The new prisoners were ill-treated - housed in filthy conditions, force-fed if they refused to eat and, in some cases, physically abused. As news of the suffragettes' poor treatment at the facility leaked out to the public, support for their cause grew and contributed to women winning the right to vote in 1920.

The reform experiment ended shortly thereafter and bars and cells were built at Occoquan as the facility expanded to over 3,000 acres housing more than 7,000 inmates - far beyond its capacity. The outdated facility finally closed in 2001 sending 2,440 acres to Fairfax County, 400 of which were used for this spacious park along the river.

Fairfax
Phone Number - (703) 690-2121
Website - www.nvrpa.org/occoquan.html
Admission Fee - None
Park Hours - Dawn to dusk; closes after Thanksgiving for the winter
Directions - Exit off I-95 onto Route 123 North and follow 1.5 miles to the park entrance on right.

The Walks

Hiking is clearly not the recreation star at Occoquan - there are no trail maps and it takes a sharp eye to spot the trailheads but remain dogged in your determination to get your dog on the trail here and you wil be rewarded. You will find a Virginia state *Bird and Wildlife Trail* in the woods on the left just past the boat ramp, next to an elevated picnic shelter.

It begins as a desultory affair, slogging uphill on a paw-unfriendly stony road and when the trail leaves the road it gets downright wild and wooly on a narrow, overgrown path. You'll even find the trail studded with long-ago discarded bricks. But stick with it. Soon the path opens up as it rolls aong ravines and into a stream valley. You're now traveling on pine straw in many places. The trail often looks exactly like the forest floor but is easy to follow with large blue blazes. And your dog will have no trouble sniffing out the route. Use the grassy shoulders along the park road to close your canine hiking loop.

Another hiking option is the white-blazed *Ridge Trail* that climbs a bluff overlooking the Occoquan River. Look for a set of wooden stairs and work your way back towards the park entrance. The paved multi-use trail closes this loop.

Trail Sense: The trails are easier to follow than to find.

Dog Friendliness
Dogs are allowed throughout the park.

Traffic
Most of the visitors to this busy park would be surprised to discover there were natural hiking trails here.

Canine Swimming
The boat ramp provides the easiest access to the Occoquan River for canine aquatics.

Trail Time
With some creativity, more than one hour.

34
Potomac Heritage Trail

The Park

The George Washington Memorial Parkway was developed in 1932 to commemorate the bicentennial of the first President's birth and to preserve the beauty of the Potomac River corridor.

Tucked inside the Parkway between Theodore Roosevelt Island and the American Legion Bridge is the *Potomac Heritage Trail*, a segment of the *Potomac Heritage National Scenic Trail* that is a 425-mile corridor of trails between the Chesapeake Bay and Allegheny Highlands.

The Walks

This 10-mile linear riverwalk can be broken into manageable chunks with the numerous access points to the trail. Of course, the trail from parks such as Potomac Overlook Park, Gulf Branch Nature Center and Turkey Run Park to the PHT can be a hike in themselves.

This canine hike can be a cracking good adventure for your dog. The floodplain path is often muddy and there will be several stream crossings that must be made, and after heavy rains will be impassable (the highest recorded level of the river reached 15 feet above the trail in 1936). You will encounter steep passages that will set you and your dog to panting. Most of the trail is under a steady parade of thick shade trees. It is easy to forget that you are just across the river from the nation's capital - although you will not escape the noise of traffic and airplanes heading for Reagan National Airport.

Trail Sense: Brochures and maps will help you plan your canine hiking day; out on the trail it is blazed.

Fairfax/Arlington

Phone Number
- None

Website
- www.nps.gov/archive/gwmp/vapa/pht.htm

Admission Fee
- None

Park Hours
- Sunrise to sunset

Directions
- Several trailheads off the George Washington Memorial Parkway between Theodore Roosevelt Island and the American Legion Bridge.

Dog Friendliness

Dogs are allowed along the route of the trail.

Traffic

More than nine million people a year visit the parks along the George Washington Memorial Parkway but few of those actually come down to the Potomac Heritage Trail. Bikes are not permitted on any part of the trail.

Canine Swimming

Carefully allow your dog in the Potomac River.

Trail Time

With a car shuttle, the trail can be completed in a half-day.

35
Hidden Oaks
Nature Center

The Park

This small 52-acre sanctuary is squeezed into the heart of Fairfax County, just inside the Beltway. The urban woodland forest features a vibrant diversity of plant and animal species thriving in a green oasis.

The Walks

The feature trail at Hidden Oaks is a 1/3-mile, wood-chip-covered interpretive *Old Oak Trail* around the nature center. The average oak, by the way, will drop about 5,000 acorns a year but less than 50 will sprout and half of those will die.

For additional canine hiking you can take your dog into the Accotink Creek stream valley where the dirt trail crosses the water three times. There is modest elevation gain on this trail but nothing close to setting your dog to panting. The trails are wide and airy in the woods below the nature center.

Trail Sense: An interpretive brochure with trail map is available outside the nature center building.

Fairfax

Phone Number
- (703) 941-1065

Website
- www.fairfaxcounty.gov/parks/hiddenoaks/

Admission Fee
- None

Park Hours
- Grounds open dawn to dusk

Directions
- Take Beltway Exit 52B which is Little River Turnpike or Route 236 east to the first traffic light at Hummer Road. Turn left on Hummer Road and then left at the park entrance.

Dog Friendliness

Dogs are welcome at the Hidden Oaks Nature Center and the water fountain includes a spout for dogs.

Traffic

Foot traffic only and not much of it.

Canine Swimming

The Accotink Creek is only deep enough for splashing.

Trail Time

Less than one hour.

"My dog can bark like a Congressman, fetch like an aide,
beg like a press secretary and play dead like a receptionist."
-Gerald Solomon

36
John Marshall Birthplace Park

The Park

Although less than 200 acres, Mountain Meadow Preserve packs a lot of diversity into your canine hike with little purchase. Former farm fields have transitioned into wildflower meadows and grasslands - you can still spot abandoned farm machinery on the property.

The surrounding hills supported a gravel operation in the middle of the 20th century amela Weatherbee is a consulting botanist and author of "Flora of Berkshire County", a complete list of county plants, with chapters on geology, plant communities, plant geography, climate, botanical history and land use history. She has conducted studies of the plants of Kampoosa Bog, Mount Greylock, Pleasant Valley and other areas of the Berkshires. She has been a member of the Advisory Committee for nine years.

Fauquier

Phone Number
- None

Website
- www.dgif.state.va.us/wildlife/vbwt/site.asp?trail=3&site=PCU06&loop=PCU

Admission Fee
- None

Park Hours
- Sunrise to sunset

Directions
- The park is southeast of Warrenton. Take Route 643, Meetze Road, to its end at Route 28 (Catlett Road). Make a right and then left on Germantown Road (Route 649). The park is on the left, just past the railroad tracks.

The Walks

You can take your dog on a short country lane hike along a branch of Licking Run. Listen to the cows and watch the corn sway in the breeze. You'll pass through a wildflower meadow and reach the stone memorial marking the location of Marshall's birthplace.

You won't learn much about John Marshall on this outing but it is more of a place to reflect on where he was and where we are.

Trail Sense: The old farm road leads directly to the memorial.

Dog Friendliness
Dogs are allowed to visit the birthplace of John Marshall.
Traffic
None.
Canine Swimming
None.
Trail Time
Less than one hour.

As a young lawyer, 19th century Senator George Graham Vest of Missouri, addressed the jury on behalf of his client, suing a neighbor who had killed his dog. Vest's speech has come to be known as "Tribute to the Dog."

The best friend a man has in the world may turn against him and become his enemy. His son or daughter that he has reared with loving care may prove ungrateful. Those who are nearest and dearest to us, those whom we trust with our happiness and our good name may become traitors to their faith. The money that a man has, he may lose. It flies away from him, perhaps when he needs it most. A man's reputation may be sacrificed in a moment of ill-considered action. The people who are prone to fall on their knees to do us honor when success is with us may be the first to throw the stone of malice when failure settles its cloud upon our heads. The one absolutely unselfish friend that man can have in this selfish world, the one that never deserts him, the one that never proves ungrateful or treacherous is his dog. A man's dog stands by him in prosperity and in poverty, in health and in sickness. He will sleep on the cold ground, where the wintry winds blow and the snow drives fiercely, if only he may be near his master's side. He will kiss the hand that has no food to offer; he will lick the wounds and sores that come in an encounter with the roughness of the world. He guards the sleep of his pauper master as if he were a prince. When all other friends desert, he remains. When riches take wings, and reputation falls to pieces, he is as constant in his love as the sun in its journey through the heavens. If fortune drives the master forth an outcast in the world, friendless and homeless, the faithful dog asks no higher privilege than that of accompanying him, to guard him against danger, to fight against his enemies. And when the last scene of all comes, and death takes his master in its embrace and his body is laid away in the cold ground, no matter if all other friends pursue their way, there by the graveside will the noble dog be found, his head between his paws, his eyes sad, but open in alert watchfulness, faithful and true even in death.

37
Pohick Bay Regional Park
Fairfax County
On Gunston Road (Route 242) off Route 1 on Mason Neck

Most outings to Mason Neck with your dog will wind up in the state park or national wildlife refuge but you may want to make a stop in this expansive recreation and camping park along the Pohick Bay as well. There are about four miles of wide, level bridle trails your dog will share with the occasional horse.

You'll be exploring a typical Eastern deciduous forest on flat, easy-trotting terrain. In places you'll touch on Pohick Bay for superior swimming for your dog. Dogs are also allowed in the campground. Bluebird nesting boxes have been scattered around the park's 1,000 acres with sparse ground cover - you can recognize an artificial bluebird home because there is no perch.

38
Hidden Pond Nature Center
Fairfax County
In Springfield; from Fairfax County Parkway (Route 7100) to Old Keene Mill Road (Route 644) and right on Greeley Boulevard

Nothing strenuous in store for your dog here - just quiet trails centered around a small, tranquil pond. The groomed paths trace streams and wetlands in this wooded oasis. Although only 25 acres, a half-mile trail leads to the 700-acre Pohick Stream Valley Park. Here is plenty of trotting on the suburban park's linear trails.

39
Franklin Park

Loudoun County

West of Purcellville on Tranquility Rod off of Main Street (Business Route 7)

Former dairy farms are the bedrock for this 203-acre park favored for its views of the Blue Ridge Mountains. Most of the park is given over to sports and recreation but two perimeter trails over three miles long circumnavigate the property. The *Inner Trail* is used mostly by equestrians so visiting canine hikers will want to set off on the *Outer Trail*.

Most of the marked paths are wide open across the rolling hills but the trail dips into natural areas along the way. Keep your dog out of the sports complex and off the playing fields and playground.

40
Colvin Run Mill Park/Difficult Run Trail

Fairfax County

On Colvin Run Mill Road five miles west of Tysons Corner on Leesburg Pike (Route 7)

Colvin Run Mill, envisioned by George Washington, was built in 1811 and has been restored to working order. The park is a good launching spot for the long-distance *Difficult Run Trail*. Fairfax County banned the building of homes in floodplains and that enabled the construction of this 15-mile linear path rom the heart of the county to the mouth of Difficult Run into rapids on the Potomac River.

Heading north, the terrain is gentler than setting out in the southerly direction. Parking at the northern terminus is on Georgetown Pike (Route 193) and at the south in Oak Marr County Park off Jermantown Road. Well-marked at the trailheads, like its name, this route can be difficult to follow. Connecting trails and streets can be used to create canine circuit hikes if a car shuttle is not available.

41
Lake Fairfax Park
Fairfax County
Turn left on Baron Cameron Avenue from Leesburg Pike (Route 7) to the second left on Lake Fairfax Drive

The lake and waterpark are stars here but a dogged canine hiker can find a reason to visit. A mostly natural trail leaves from behind the park office and climbs across the dam towards the campground as it ducks in an out of shaded woods. Exit through Loop C where you find a sign for the *Nature Trail*. Your dog will be stepping through some streams as you head towards the residential developments and onto part of the Reston Paths.

You can also pick up the *Buttermilk Creek Nature Trail* that leaves the park for a trot down an old dairy farm road and cow path. This curvilinear trail runs for just short of a mile through meadows and forests. Soapstone and serpentine were once mined here and you still may find bits of minerals along the route here.

42
Fred Crabtree Park (formerly Fox Mill District Park)
Fairfax County
Southwest of Reston on Fox Mill Road (Route 665), east of John Herrity Parkway

This suburban retreat, named for Fred Crabtree who worked to acquire land for two score baseball fields in the county, is about evenly divided between active recreation and thick woods. There are enough twists and turns and interconnecting natural surface trails in this small greenspace to attract the interest of dirt bikers as well as your dog.

Shortly from the parking lot your dog will be immeresed in shady woods where streams and rocks are featured. If you head south you will soon be working up steep grades and by the time you return to the parking lot your dog will have scored a spirited workout.

43
Wakefield Park
Fairfax County
Off Braddock Road (Route 620), just west of the Capital Beltway (I-495) Exit 54

Most of the trails in this hourglass-shaped, 292-acre park are in the northern end and get most of their use from cross-country runners and mountain bikes. These may be the most heavily-used mountain bike trails in Northern Virginia. If that isn't enough to dissuade you, it is a healthy canine hike just to reach the trail system with your dog.

The *Upland Loop* that squeezes against the Beltway in the southern half of Wakefield is a better choice if you bring your dog to this park. Also the *Cross County Trail* that dreams of connecting the Potomac River to the Occoquan River comes through Wakefield for about two miles on asphalt, stonedust and dirt. You can use the *Creek Trail* that hugs Accotink Creek to form large canine hiking loops with the Cross County.

44
Dyke Marsh
Fairfax County
South of Alexandria on the Potomac River; accessible from the George Washington Parkway at Belle Haven

Since 1973 the National Park Service has managed the Dyke Marsh Preserve as the last major remnant of formerly extensive freshwater tidal marshes along the Potomac. In the early 1800s earthen walls were built around the perimeter of the marsh to create cropland, hence the name. Today's marsh is holding at about 380 acres.

The trail leading into the wetlands is called the *Haul Road* and is a favorite of birdwatchers, nature lovers and dog owners on the hunt for a quiet outing in an otherwise bustling area. More than 300 species of birds and over 300 species of plants have been recorded in Dyke Marsh. This canine hike is conducted mostly under the shade of a floodplain forest - and don't forget the bug spray.

45
George Hellwig Memorial Park
Prince William County
North of the Quantico Marine Corps Base at the intersection of Bristow Road (Route 619) and Dumfires Road (Route 234)

In 1982, the Samsky family gave land to the Prince William Park Authority for a park at Independent Hill. Citizens requested that the park be named for George Hellwig, an outstanding local citizen who lived nearby.

The canine hiking in this spread-out park takes place across the 32-station *Fitness Trail*. The loop is completely under light, airy woods on a crushed stone path. The terrain rolls slightly and the well-groomed path is wide enough to hike comfortably with a small pack of dogs. The stream beds are usually dry and there is no swimming available for your dog in the park.

46
Algonkian Regional Park

Loudoun County

On the Potomac River in Sterling; off Cascades Parkway from Route 7

Algonkian Park features easy canine hiking across 800 acres of flat Potomac River floodplain. Most of the park is given over to recreational activities, principally a waterpark and a golf course, through which the paved park trail travels. In the western section of the park your dog can enter into light woods on a rooty, dirt nature trail for the better part of two miles. If you are a fan of whitetail deer, come to the park in the evenings with your dog.

There are plenty of grassy fields for you to informally hike with your dog in the open air without crossing the golf course. Nearby you can stop at the boat ramp for extended play in the waters of the Potomac River.

47
South Run District Park

Fairfax County

South of Springfield off Fairfax County Parkway, just east of Lee Chapel Road

South Run is better known for its recreation center and playing fields but there is a slice of woodland that contains the *Spartan Trail*. This flat, linear trail can provide almost an hour of canine hiking. Paved trails connect South Run with Burke Lake Park and Lake Mercer.

At the trailhead near the park entrance is an off-leash dog park for your dog to sample after the hike. It is a large fenced enclosure with some shade around the edges but not much grass.

48
Lake Accotink Park

Fairfax County

West of Springfield on Accotink Park Road off Highland Avenue; from I-95 take Old Keene Mill Road west and turn right on Hanover Avenue

This thickly wooded neighborhood park is centered on a 70-acre lake that features a mostly flat trail with an occasional hill leading to lake views. A 3.75-mile circle trail surrounds the lake and the Accotink Creek; spurs lead off into various neighborhoods and north to Wakefield Park. Mile markers are posted on both sides of the lake.

The is mostly easy-going on dirt and crushed gravel but you will be sharing the trail with plenty of bikes and other users. Less crowded canine hiking can be had in the mostly unmarked trail system south of the lake.

A few times each summer your dog can board a pontoon boat for a special cruise around Lake Accotink.

49
Jones Point Park

Arlington County

In Alexandria on the Potomac River off Washington Street under the Woodrow Wilson Bridge

The first cornerstone for the southern boundary of the District of Columbia was laid on the Potomac River shoreline here in 1801. In 1855, the Jones Point Lighthouse was built as the first inland waterway lighthouse in the United States. The light guided ships across shoals in the river until 1926. The steel tower for the light has been torn down but the small lighthouse remains.

A shipyard operated here during World War I but when it became obsolete the area was neglected until it became an Arlington city park. There are large swaths of greenspace for your dog, short wooded trails and the Potomac River for a canine swimming pool.

50
Fort Hunt Park
Fairfax County
South of Alexandria off the George Washington Memorial Parkway at the exit marked "Fort Hunt Road/Fort Hunt Park"

The military history of this old farmland began during the Spanish American War when a coastal fortification was built here. During World War II Fort Hunt was the site for top secret military intelligence operations where captured German sailors were interrogated. Today it is primarily a picnic park.

There are no formal trails for your dog here but many canine hikers use the pedestrian lane of the circular park road for an invigorating outing. There are plenty of open spaces for a game of fetch or a free-form canine hike. Fort Hunt has a few concrete bunkers remaining to explore but no swimming for your dog.

Camping With Your Dog In Northern Virginia

Bull Run Regional Park Campground
Fairfax County
North of Manassas; take I-66 to Exit 52 (Route 29) at Centerville and drive two miles south and turn left on Bull Run Post Office Road and follow signs.
tent and RV   (703) 631-0550

Burke Lake Park Campground
Fairfax County
South of Fairfax; from I-66 take the Fairfax County Parkway, Exit 55A (7100 South towards Springfield). Go 5 miles and turn right on Burke Lake Road. Turn left on Ox Road (Route 123) to the park entrance on the left.
tent and RV   (703) 323-6600

Greenville Farm Family Campground
Prince William County
North of Haymarket; From I-66 take Exit 40 and go four miles north on Route 15. Make a right on Route 234 and quickly left on Shelter Lane (Route 601).
tent and RV   (703) 754-7944

Hillwood Camping Park
Prince William County
At 14222 Lee Highway (Route 29) in Gainesville; from I-66 take Exit 43A and the entrance is onemile on the right.
RV only   (703) 754-6105

Lake Fairfax Park Campground
Fairfax County
In Reston; leave the Beltway (I-495) on Exit 47A to Route 7 (Leesburg Pike) west to a left on Baron Cameron Avenue to the second left on Lake Fairfax Drive.
tent and RV   (703) 471-5415

Pohick Bay Regional Park Campground
Fairfax County
On Mason Neck; take I-95 and exit at Lorton. Turn left on Lorton Road, right on Armistead Road, right on Route 1 and left on Gunston Road to park on left.
tent and RV   (703) 339-6104

Prince William Forest Park - Oak Ridge Campground
Prince William County
West of Dumfries; take I-95 south to exit 150-B (VA Route 619/Joplin Road). The park entrance is the second right.
tent and RV   (703) 221-5843

Prince William Travel Trailer Village
Prince William County
Near Dumfries; from I-95 take Exit 152B for Manassas and go 2.5 miles to the campground on the left.
RV only   (703) 221-2474

Your Dog At The Beach

It is hard to imagine many places a dog is happier than at a beach. Whether running around on the sand, jumping in the water or just lying in the sun, every dog deserves a day at the beach. But all too often dog owners stopping at a sandy stretch of beach are met with signs designed to make hearts - human and canine alike - droop: NO DOGS ON BEACH. Below are rules for taking your dog on a day trip to an Atlantic Ocean or Chesapeake Bay beach on the Delmarva Peninsula (*from north to south*).

Delaware:

Delaware State Law prohibits dogs from all swimming and sunbathing beaches from May 1 to September 30.
You may also find restrictions on beaches that have been designated as shorebird nesting areas. Otherwise:

ATLANTIC OCEAN

Lewes/ Cape Henlopen
From May 1 to September 30 no dogs are allowed on the beach between 8:00 am and 6:30 pm

Rehoboth Beach
Dogs are prohibited from the beach and boardwalk from April 1 to October 31

Dewey Beach
Dogs are not allowed on the beach between 9:30 am to 5:30 pm in season

Delaware Seashore
Dogs are allowed on the beach in designated areas year-round; not on swimming beaches or Rehoboth Bay at Tower Road from May 1 to September 30

Bethany Beach
No dogs on the beach or boardwalk from April 1 to October 1

Fenwick Island
No dogs permitted on the beach from May 1 to September 30

Kitts Hummock   Private

North Bowers   Dogs allowed anytime; a wide, long sand
            beach with plenty of pebbles

Big Stone Beach   Dogs allowed anytime; a remote and
                  desolate beach with good waves and little
         parking

Slaughter Beach Dogs allowed anytime with beach access
         at small lots between residences;
                        a sheltered, flat beach with little wave
                        action

Fowler Beach   Dogs allowed anytime and this is one of
         the best places in Delaware to bring a
                  dog; no development and backed by
                  dunes, this is the bay beach that most
                  resembles an ocean beach, the sloping
                  beach promotes excellent wave action
         and you can walk for hours

Prime Hook Beach   Private

Broadkill Beach   Dogs allowed anytime; good wave action
         for canine swimming and plenty of room
to hike up and down

Maryland:

Assateague Island   Dogs allowed on the beach but not on
National Seashore   the trails

Assateague State   Dogs are not allowed in the park
Park

Ocean City   Dogs are allowed on the beach and
                       boardwalk from October 1 to April 30

Tips For Taking Your Dog To The Beach

- The majority of dogs can swim and love it, but dogs entering the water for the first time should be tested; never throw a dog into the water. Start in shallow water and call your dog's name - or try to coax him in with a treat or toy. Always keep your dog within reach.

- Another way to introduce your dog to the water is with a dog that already swims and is friendly with your dog. Let your dog follow his friend.

- If your dog begins to doggie paddle with his front legs only, lift his hind legs and help him float. He should quickly catch on and will keep his back end up.

- Swimming is a great form of exercise, but don't let your dog overdo it. He will be using new muscles and may tire quickly.

- Be careful of strong tides that are hazardous for even the best swimmers.

- Cool ocean water is tempting to your dog. Do not allow him to drink too much sea water. Salt in the water will make him sick. Salt and other minerals found in the ocean can damage your dog's coat so regular bathing is essential.

- Check with a lifeguard for daily water conditions - dogs are easy targets for jellyfish and sea lice.

- Dogs can get sunburned, especially short-haired dogs and ones with pink skin and white hair. Limit your dog's exposure when the sun is strong and apply sunblock to his ears and nose 30 minutes before going outside.

- If your dog is out of shape, don't encourage him to run on the sand, which is strenuous exercise and a dog that is out of shape can easily pull a tendon or ligament.

Doggin The Chesapeake Bay

The Chesapeake Bay is one of our great recreation destinations (*www.baygateways.net*). More than 1 in every 15 Americans live within a short drive of the nation's largest estuary and millions come each year for the sailing, the lighthouses, the Atlantic Blue Crabs... What about for your dog? Some of the best Maryland state parks on the Bay don't allow dogs (Calvert Cliffs, Sandy Point) but there are some fine beaches to take your dog to nonetheless in Virginia and Maryland. Here are the ten best -

1.   KIPTOPEKE STATE PARK (*Virginia, eastern shore*)
Features more than a half-mile of wide sandy beaches, backed by dunes. Offshore nine concrete World War II surplus ships have been sunk as a breakwater, leaving gentle waves for your dog to play in. Also an easy 1.5-mile *Baywoods Trail* when you want to take a break from the water. Dogs are welcome in the campground.

2.   FIRST LANDING STATE PARK (*Virginia, south mouth of Bay*)
One of the finest state parks you'll find anywhere features an ocean-type beach at the mouth of the Chesapeake Bay. You can easily hike with your dog for over an hour on the beach with views of the Chesapeake Bay Bridge Tunnel and ocean-going vessels in view the entire time.

3.   TERRAPIN PARK (*Maryland, eastern shore at Bay Bridge*)
Terrapin Park has over 4,000 feet of beach frontage at the tip of Kent Island. Your dog will enjoy frisky waves and canine swimming in the north shadow of the Bay Bridge. The trail to the beach takes you across oyster chaff.

4.   DOWNS MEMORIAL PARK (*Maryland, western shore north of Annapolis*)
Looking for a dog-friendly park? At Downs Memorial Park there is a "pet parking" stall outside the information center. A dog drinking bowl is chained to a human water fountain. Best of all is Dog Beach, an isolated, scruffy 40-yard stretch of sand where you can let the dog off leash for canine aquatics in the Chesapeake Bay. The wave action is just right for dogs and there is enough sand for digging. Need we say more?

5.   FLAG PONDS NATURE PARK(*Maryland, western shore - Lusby*)
Thick woods and an isolated sandy beach backed by wild grasses are prime attractions but don't come too early - the park doesn't open until 9:00 a.m and is only open Memorial Day to Labor Day daily and weekends all year round.

6.   MATAPEAKE PARK (*Maryland, eastern shore, south of Bay Bridge*)
This small park on the Chesapeake Bay features a pleasant one-mile wood-chip trail through a pine forest but the reason to come here is a stretch of sandy beach where your dog is welcome off-leash. The beach is a bit too industrial for sunbathers which makes it the perfect place for dogs to romp. Matapeake Park is just south of the Bay Bridge with splendid views of the bay and bridge.

7.   WYE ISLAND NATURAL RESOURCES MANAGEMENT
       AREA (*Maryland, eastern shore*)
The *Ferry Landing Trail* was once the only access road to the island, lined with Osage Orange trees imported to serve as a natural fence. Osage orange trees originated in a small region of Texas, Oklahoma and Arkansas, which was home to the Osage Indians, who used its wood for bows. This mile-long path ends at a small, sandy beach.

8.   POINT LOOKOUT STATE PARK (*Maryland, southern tip of western shore*)
A Civil War prison to hold Confederate soldiers was built here at the mouth of the Potomac River and is the main attraction of the park but dogs aren't allowed here. Before crossing the causeway to the island, however, is a small, sandy dog beach with excellent wave action.

9.   EASTERN NECK NATIONAL WILDLIFE REFUGE
       (*Maryland, eastern shore, south of Rock Hall*)
Technically the secluded sandy beach at the end of the *Boxes Point Trail* is on the Chester River but your dog won't quibble when she tests these fun waves.

10.   NORTH POINT STATE PARK (*Maryland, western shore, east of Baltimore*)
Although only 20 acres in size, the Bay Shore Park was considered one of the finest amusement parks ever built along the Chesapeake Bay. Opened in 1906, the park featured an Edwardian-style dance hall, bowling alley and restaurant set in among gardens and curving pathways. There were rides such as a water toboggan and Sea Swing. Visitors would travel to the shore from Baltimore on a trolley line. Your dog can explore the remains and dive in the Chesapeake at a small wading beach at the Visitor Center.

Index To Parks and Open Spaces

Made in the USA
Lexington, KY
07 April 2012